ISRAEL: THE MYSTERY OF PEACE

This is an important book for all those who long to see the peace of Jerusalem and the reconciliation of Jew and Arab. R.T. Kendall's powerful rejection of Replacement Theology is particularly significant.

The Rev Dr Clifford Hill
The Centre for Biblical and Hebraic studies,
Moggerhanger

ISRAEL: THE MYSTERY OF PEACE

True Stories Demonstrating God's Road Map for Peace in Israel Today

Julia Fisher

Authentic
LIFESTYLE

First published 2004 by Authentic Lifestyle

10 09 08 07 06 05 04   7 6 5 4 3 2 1
Authentic Lifestyle is an imprint of Authentic Media,
9 Holdom Avenue, Bletchley, Milton Keynes, Bucks,
MK1 1QR, UK
and PO Box 1047, Waynesboro GA 30830-2047, USA.

British Library Cataloguing in Publication Data
A catalogue record for this book is available from the British
Library

1-86024-297-9

Cover design by James Kessell
Print Management by Adare Carwin
Printed and Bound in Denmark by Nørhaven Paperback

ACKNOWLEDGEMENTS

My thanks to all those who have shared their stories in this book believing the time is now right to do so; to R.T. Kendall for his kind encouragement and contribution; to Malcolm Down for believing in this book enough to publish it; and to Norman, my husband, for his understanding as he has watched this project develop, for his companionship as we have travelled together to Israel and for his willingness to share in the journey.

CONTENTS

FOREWORD

Discerning God's agenda is a process that needs to be approached with a high degree of caution and more than a pinch of humility. If the Spirit 'blows wherever it pleases' who are we to attempt to determine or even predict such activity? God has given us his Word and his Spirit to lead us into truth. The purpose of this book is not so much to interpret the words of Scripture but to suggest ways in which the wind may be blowing and to see whether possibly, tentatively, events that are largely hidden from public gaze might indicate a pattern that would enable us prayerfully to trim our sails in harmony with God's plans and to move with the Spirit.

Having lived in Israel for almost fourteen years, eight of those as Rector of Christ Church, Jerusalem, it has been my privilege to meet a broad spectrum of the leadership of the body of the Messiah in the land, whether Messianic, Arab/Palestinian or international. In doing so I have met most of those whose stories Julia shares so movingly in this book. I have witnessed the hopes and aspirations, as well as the disappointments and suffering of faithful men and women who are serving their Lord and his people with such integrity of heart and mind. The clarion ring of truth and love is certainly being sounded out in these stories.

A 'Road Map' to be effective must be readable but also indicate faithfully the facts on the ground. Many may feel that a politically drawn map runs the danger of leaving out the contour lines of God's purposes and will, therefore, almost inevitably, fail to achieve a positive outcome.

On the other hand, the Alexandria Declaration is a process, begun by Lord Carey before he retired as Archbishop of Canterbury, which seeks to draw in the religious dimension in the Middle East conflict and to harness this influence to find an effective solution. This is to be applauded and is a track that Christian people will want to endorse.

But is it only in such overt ways that an effective road map to peace is to be found? *Israel: The Mystery of Peace* may be likened to the search for hidden treasure, following a trail of clues. Perhaps the authority of this book derives from its telling of some of those unlikely ways in which the Holy Spirit is working. If there is a common ingredient it is to be seen in a powerful mix of love, faith and prayer, coupled with an understanding of God's continuing purposes for his old covenant people. Perhaps this is a strand of biblical teaching, witness the numerous promises to the Jewish people, that the wider church could do well once more to embrace if it is to begin to understand what God is doing at this time.

Julia Fisher has done us a service in allowing us to catch these glimpses. In reading this book my prayer is that we may be attentive to the Holy Spirit and be ready to be stirred within, beyond the apparent scope of such a modest book.

Revd Ray Lockhart
Bath, England
August 2003

CHAPTER 1

FROM LONDON TO JERUSALEM

Israel: The Mystery of Peace is a collection of rather bizarre stories! Put them side-by-side, however, and you will see that a mysterious thread runs through them. The hypothesis of the book is that there is peace in the Holy Land between Jews and Arabs today.

But, you may say, how can I be so sure when it is also obvious that Israel is a war-torn land where people are dying daily and a sense of hopelessness hangs like a cloud over the country? I agree with you! However, I have seen this peace with my own eyes and spoken to those concerned. These true stories are here as proof that something is quietly happening that currently not many people realise: a peace movement is gaining momentum in Israel that will soon take the world by storm.

So if you are one of those people who are puzzled about what is going on in the Middle East; if you wonder what all the fuss is over Jerusalem; if you're tired of political rhetoric from Zionists on the one hand and militant Islamic fundamentalists on the other; if you wonder whether or not Israel is 'special' to God, whether Arabs have a role in his 'plan', or whether the Jews are still his 'chosen people', this book is for you.

I stumbled across these stories almost by accident.

In 1998, I was having a conversation with Olave Snelling, one of my fellow presenters at Premier Radio's London studios. We were talking about the need some women have to get away from home and family for a short, inspiring break, to be able to pray and meet with like-minded people. As we talked, Olave had the idea of a holiday for women, a time when they could travel somewhere exciting and at the same time pray together and be taught the Bible. Our discussion progressed and the idea of a tour to Israel for women was born – 'Women of the Book'. Olave led the first tour in June 1998 and I led the second in November of the same year.

Being a tour leader was a new experience. I had fifty women on the trip from all walks of life and from many nationalities – it was fantastic. Never let anyone tell you that holidays for women are dull: they are not!

But it was on the plane home that something unexpected occurred. Although very tired, I was relieved that we had enjoyed a successful tour and were now heading back to London with fifty happy ladies. And then it happened. Just as I was dozing off to sleep it was as though somebody spoke to me. 'Wake up, Julia. Write this down.' In an instant I was fully alert and reaching for my notepad. 'In six weeks you will be back in Israel. You have seen the land and visited the sites but I am bringing you back because I want you to tell the stories of what it means to be a believer in Israel today.'

Was I imagining this? There was only one way to find out, and that was to wait and see if it happened. I didn't tell anybody about this. And it did happen.

My 'Mission'

The invitation to go back to Israel arrived almost imme-diately. IGTO (the Israeli Government Tourist Office) was inviting journalists on a press trip to see the new hotels, tourist sites and other arrangements that were being put in place for the millennium. Israel was expecting that during the year 2000, the usual number of tourists would increase from one million to three million – and they wanted to show us that they were ready to welcome the crowds.

The trip was planned for early February 1999, and despite a fairly hectic schedule I was able to clear a couple of days at either end to start my 'research'.

But where should I begin and with whom? I didn't know anybody in Israel well enough to ask for their help. I didn't even know what the state of the church there was, let alone how many believers lived in the land.

I started to read articles by Christians who worked there and one issue in particular caught my imagination – reconciliation. Now this was before the current *intifada* had begun, but even so, I was reading some intriguing stories of Jewish/Arab initiatives and Christian/Jewish projects.

As the date for my departure drew closer I heard on the grapevine that a breakfast meeting for pastors in Jerusalem was scheduled for the morning after I was to arrive. But I didn't know anybody. How could I get to meet these people? All I could do was pray and wait for God to lead me to the person who would open the door. If this sounds as though I was quite nonchalant, let me assure you, I was finding it hard to trust God in this way and at such a late hour. To be honest, I was saying to the Lord 'Why choose me?'

Then the first glimmer of a breakthrough came. On the night before I was due to leave, the phone rang.

'Julia, there's a man called Ray Lockhart on your plane to Tel Aviv tomorrow. He's the rector at Christ Church and knows many of the Christian leaders in Jerusalem.

Here's his number; he's staying in London tonight at his daughter's home.'

Poor Ray! To have a call from a radio journalist asking to meet him at Heathrow the next day – he had every reason to say no. But he didn't.

'How will I recognise you?' he asked.

'I have a yellow suitcase!'

Ray found me at the airport and as we chatted he asked me what my 'mission' was. I told him simply what had happened. He could have discounted my story because, let's be honest, there are some crazy Christians who get a 'thing' about Israel. In fact, there's a ward for them in a Jerusalem psychiatric hospital: the condition is called 'Jerusalem syndrome'.

We chatted for a couple of hours as we waited to board our plane. Ray listened attentively and then said, 'There's a breakfast for pastors in Jerusalem at 7 o'clock tomorrow morning. They don't usually welcome visitors, especially journalists, but come and be my guest.'

I could hardly believe it and we arranged to meet outside Christ Church, by the Jaffa Gate, at 6.30 the following morning.

Early morning in Jerusalem is full of promise. The air is fresh and the light is bright. That morning, I awoke to hear sparrows chirping loudly outside my hotel window and, being in Arab East Jerusalem, I could hear the call to prayer from a nearby mosque.

Ray was chairing the meeting. Some had travelled quite a distance to be there. I think I was the only woman present. I could make out a number of languages and accents including Hebrew, Arabic, American, Canadian, German and English. I now realise that these meetings provide a valuable opportunity for the exchange of news between people who normally wouldn't meet – especially today.

Ray opened the meeting and immediately introduced me to the assembled group. 'Tell them why you're here, Julia.'

It didn't take long. I told them my story and said I would be available after the meeting if any of them felt they would like to tell me about their work.

And so it was that I started to hear what it meant to be a believer in the land of Israel. I met Dr Gershon Nirel, a Messianic Jewish believer and director of Yad Hashmona, a Messianic kibbutz-style community between Jerusalem and Tel Aviv, and Dr Salim Munayer, an Arab Christian and founder of the reconciliatory organisation Musalaha.

From that one meeting friendships have been forged, and I have been back to Israel many, many times. Then the *intifada* began and the stories that I was researching started to take on a whole new meaning. Reconciliation between enemies is, I have observed, only for the brave.

As well as meeting believers involved in reconciliation between Jews and Arabs and Jews and Christians in the Holy Land today, I have also found my thinking influenced by certain verses in the Bible. These have convinced me that the relevance of Jewish and Gentile believers coming together at this time in our history is no accident but is actually God's plan. For example, the letter Paul wrote to the Ephesians mentions 'God's secret plan' to reconcile Jew and Gentile. He wrote of how 'God's purpose was to show his wisdom in all its rich variety to all the rulers and authorities in the heavenly realms. They will see this when Jews and Gentiles are joined together in his church' (Eph. 3:10).

Was I witnessing something in Israel today that had not happened since the early church started two thousand years ago? The realisation of this started to dawn on me and the stories in this book began to emerge. Yes, the numbers of believers in the Holy Land are relatively small. Yes, the people are challenged to their core: the pressure on both Jewish believers and Arab Christians from their own communities, let alone from outside, is sometimes overwhelming. But reconciliation is happening, and it is happening in greater and greater numbers.

Something is quietly occurring in the Holy Land today that has nothing to do with politics but everything to do with the Holy Spirit. It involves Gentile Christians acting as catalysts between Jews and Arabs; Jewish and Arab believers in Jesus uniting and realising that they share a common faith in their Messiah which enables them to transcend politics, overcome their prejudice and distrust, and enjoy a peaceful coexistence. They believe that Jesus is returning to his church – a Jewish/Gentile church. This is not a popular view; many Christians would vehemently disagree. But for those involved in this movement, this is their understanding of what the Bible says. And it would appear from the evidence to date that the peace being forged is genuine and is withstanding the heat and pressure from the political climate around them.

This book is written to introduce you to some of these people. None of them are famous. None have a big, powerful organisation behind them. But the story of what they are doing – or to be more correct, what God is quietly doing through them – deserves to be told.

I visited them all during 2002, at a time when trouble and tension, suicide bombings and terrorism were happening daily. Many people were dying. Tourism had declined to an all-time low, as had the level of the Sea of Galilee as a result of a lack of rain. The country was gripped by a sense of despair – all hopes of a peaceful settlement between the Israeli government and the Palestinian Authority had been dashed. Many attempts at reconciliation and peacemaking had failed, especially in the political arena, yet these people's work was flourishing. I was seeing something good emerging from the chaos. I was witnessing at first hand reconciliation, unity and cooperation between Jew and Arab.

What follows are five true stories of triumph over adversity told by the people themselves. I have sat and talked with the people I am about to introduce you to. Often I have travelled with them. I have felt the intensity of their feelings and listened to the conviction that drives them on. What follows may challenge your view of politics, or your theology.

I have travelled to Israel on a number of occasions with R.T. Kendall, minister of Westminster Chapel in London until his recent retirement. On one of our trips in 2002 he met with Yasser Arafat, Chairman of the Palestinian Liberation Organisation, in his bombed-out headquarters in Ramallah. You can read his story at the end of the book: it shows that God sometimes moves in mysterious ways! Being a theologian, R.T. then gives a biblical perspective on these strange and curious events that I hope will help you to review, or consider for the first time, the strategic spiritual importance of what is happening today in Israel.

Maybe the world is about to see God do something in the Middle East that will surprise even the most sceptical. Once again the Jewish people are being vilified by certain political and religious ideologies that want them eradicated from the face of the earth. At the same time, the Palestinians are widely seen as being Islamic fundamentalists, so the Christian voice within this Arab community is barely heard. All the average Israeli man on the street wants is peace. Likewise his Arab neighbour. But it seems to elude them both. However, does God have a plan? Are we starting to see this plan emerging? Jesus once invited twelve ordinary men to become his disciples. They believed in him and the church has gone on expanding ever since: nothing and nobody has been able to stamp it out.

Israel: The Mystery of Peace describes some ordinary people who have responded to a prompting in their heart, resulting in some extraordinary exploits and events in Israel today.

The story begins with an American journalist, Jonathan Miles, and a trip into war-torn Gaza.

CHAPTER 2

TO GAZA WITH LOVE – THE STORY OF JONATHAN MILES

He used to be a TV journalist in America. But when I met him in 2002, he was risking his life two or three times a week to drive from Jerusalem into Gaza via the heavily guarded border crossing to bring sick and dying Palestinian children to a hospital in Tel Aviv where a Jewish medical team worked tirelessly attempting to save their lives.

So it was that in January 2002, when the *intifada* was raging, I accompanied Jonathan Miles through the Eretz crossing into Gaza from Israel, to witness for myself how one man was still able to cross a unique bridge of human-itarian aid at a time when the majority of similar bridges had collapsed.

He told me it was a dangerous mission – not many Americans venture into Gaza these days.

So who is Jonathan Miles, and how did he, a Christian from America then living in Jerusalem, come to be the catalyst between Palestinian Muslim families living in the Gaza Strip and a Jewish medical team operating in Tel Aviv?

Shevet Achim

I first read about Jonathan Miles in the *Jerusalem Post* in September 2001. He came to Israel in 1990, and as what the newspaper called a 'committed Christian Zionist' he was initially more interested in helping Jews from the former Soviet Union than in helping Palestinians.

I found him candid. Married with three children, with the fourth about to be born, he and his wife Michelle were living with his parents in America. He was working as a journalist. Anything had to be better than that, he told me.

'God called us to Israel' was how he put it.

Life must have been pretty desperate, then, if you were prepared to leave a good job in America and come to Israel on a whim?

'Well, God had to get our attention. I guess.'

His gentle banter seemed to mask a much deeper fascination with Israel than that, and, as I was to discover, the years since he left America have been dramatic and extremely costly for him and his wife and family.

Here was a man who didn't use two words when one would do. He spoke with his eyes. His mouth hardly moved when he talked. His expression was impassive, changing little. But he listens. And he watches, everything. He isn't loud and gushing. He's very quiet and, I suppose, shy. Yet I was to witness that he feels the pain of the people he meets; he seems to absorb it; take it on board. There's something refreshingly genuine about him. I've noticed this trait in other people I've met who work in situations most of us would find too uncomfortable. It's not that he's been stripped of emotion, just of sentimentality. He is not effusive. He doesn't need to be. He is doing a job where he actually does something that makes a difference to a person's life. He uses his mobile phone to call a surgeon at the Wolfson Medical Centre in Tel Aviv to request another life-saving operation. And he seems to get a real kick out of doing that. He's done this hundreds of times now. Got it down to a fine art. Developed a strong network. Built invisible bridges of trust that seem to be so strong they defy the hatred and hostility that erupt time and time again in this part of the world.

I wonder where this hatred comes from. It seems to leap out unexpectedly and terrify both communities like a huge angry black snake, its large eyes fixed on its victim. Its jaws wide open revealing rows of razor-sharp teeth that are hungry to devour the nearest unsuspecting, innocent prey. There's no time to escape. The snake seems to win every time. People on both sides hate this snake. But nobody seems able to kill it. I don't think I'm imagining it, because the medics I met at the Wolfson Medical Centre and the families in Gaza who had been there with their babies all hate this snake. It stops them going to work. It deprives them of income. It prevents them from finishing their houses. It makes them ill with worry. It tires them out with its hideous, repetitive attacks. It kills their babies.

But to return to Jonathan's story. The article I initially read about him described how, after working for a while as a volunteer helping Russian Jewish immigrants, he met a group of Israelis who were trying to raise money to help non-Jewish immigrants get urgent medical care – an encounter that was to change the course of his life. One thing led to another, and when a fellow Christian took him on a visit to the Gaza Strip, he told me how he saw for himself the crumbling health system in the Palestinian Authority. He saw desperate families with little blue babies in their arms. The irony was that help was only an hour's drive away in Tel Aviv; a short distance to travel by road but an impossible distance to travel given the political climate of unrest and lack of cooperation between the Palestinian Authority and the Israeli Government.

I read how Jonathan's own faith compelled him to do something to help these desperate people, and how, as a mark of solidarity with the Palestinian people, he decided to go and live amongst them. So, with his wife Michelle and their family of by now six children, he went to live in Rafah, one of the poorest and most isolated districts of Gaza.

Michelle takes up the story

'Initially, I had some misgivings about moving into Gaza with my young children. In fact, I was downright against it. However, I was willing to go for a trial period of three months in order to test the waters, as my husband Jonathan suggested. We moved into the overpopulated, dusty refugee camp of Rafah, on the Egyptian border. It was mid-September, and I was totally unprepared for the waves of heat that threatened to stifle me, as I struggled to adjust to the wearing of long clothing and a head-garment. I brought with me a calendar and impatiently marked off every passing day. By my calculations we would be back in Jerusalem before Christmas! I longed to have already arrived at that blessed time without having had to live and somehow painstakingly endure the months in between now and then.

'I was so opposed to prolonging our stay there that I refused to let Jonathan purchase any home appliances that would seem to imply a settling-in. Uppermost on the list of 'refuse-to-gets' was an oven. We lived on food cooked over a small, rusty, three-burner stove-top.

'Over the next three months I managed to create a disharmonious atmosphere, which rubbed off on my children and produced an ever-darkening cloud of depression and anxiety that almost swallowed us up.

'The rain season started in early December. I was sleeping in my room one night, when I was awakened by the raging winds that seemed about to blow the asbestos roofing sheets, held down by cinderblocks, off the building. As I listened to the howling tempest and the muffled, reverberating sound of the raindrops on the asbestos, I felt the Lord speaking to me. I became aware that I was making a futile attempt to run from my task, in disobedience to God's will. As I lay in my dark room I could almost imagine myself in the dark belly of the fish, as I too needed a strong jolt to awaken me from my apathetic attitude. I then knew that though I was living in the midst of the wonderful Muslims in Rafah, if I did not wish to be there, if I did not care enough about them to give up my own personal comforts, I could not have been farther away from them.

'I sprang up and ran to the office room where Jonathan was working late into the night, and told him what the Lord had shown me. The next day, while out with the girls, he bought us a new oven. The girls warned him that I would be furious! He wagered that I would not. And indeed, when they brought the oven home I accepted it with thanksgiving. With this behind me, I was ready to begin life in Rafah, and by God's grace three months became nearly five years.

'My neighbours in Rafah, although very curious to see foreigners (some of them for the first time), were also very hospitable and every day poured out their welcome and kindness. Not a day went by that we didn't have a hot bowl of food brought to our door by a sharing neighbour.

As wife and mother of the home, I was often visited by other neighbourhood mums. They would come at all hours of the day and night. This took some getting used to. But I was glad that neighbours felt comfortable to come whenever they had a need or just wanted someone to talk to. This is where my two eldest daughters helped me a great deal. They would almost always sit with me during my visits and interpret for me. While I never quite grasped Arabic with fluency, Renanah and Rebekah did so easily.

'All of us girls (with the exception of our little daughter Elly, aged 4) had to learn about 'covering' ourselves. While it wasn't mandatory for foreigners to cover their heads, we always did so whenever we went out of doors in order to show respect for our conservative Muslim friends and neighbours. This would include covering our heads with scarves, our arms with long-sleeved shirts that covered the wrist bone, and maxi-length skirts that reached below the ankle. Most often we just wore the jil-bab, a traditional Muslim dress that falls in one straight piece to the floor. This was not so easy in the high and humid heat of the summer months, but we adjusted by the grace of God. In our home, we did not cover our heads unless we had a male visitor.

'Socially, for our kids, life in the Gaza Strip had its share of challenges, but we were blessed with a healthy attitude on their part, which was 'I can do it!' By the end of our stay there, they had established some wonderful and lasting friendships. We are a home-schooling family as a rule and continued to be even in Rafah. After two years we entered our eldest daughter Renanah into the eleventh grade at the local girls' high school. After two years of studying exclusively in Arabic, she graduated second in her class, and ninth in the entire city of Rafah.

The only Christian in a Muslim school, she developed a healthy sense of who she is and what she believes.

'Our second eldest daughter, Rebekah, also entered public school in ninth grade, and is equally fluent in reading and writing both colloquial and classical Arabic.

'Joshua, our eldest son, learned to relate to young boys whose culture is quite unknown to the rest of the world. He soon discovered, however, that they are just like any other kids. They have a passion for soccer but knew nothing about baseball. So Josh set up a makeshift baseball field next to our home and amidst the rubble and barbed wire had a great time teaching the game. He learned that they also like to play 'Jews and Arabs' (their equivalent of 'Cowboys and Indians'), hide-and-seek, ping-pong, computer games: you name it, they played it. Josh also learned some interesting things from them. For example, almost all Palestinian kids know how to make their own kites from balsam wood and tissue paper. Our landlord's kids taught Josh. He also learned to play the hand drum, which most of his peers played exquisitely.

'As a family we experienced many interesting things there and we are much richer for it. I am ever thankful for the Lord's guidance in bringing us there, and opening our eyes to the lovely characteristics of the open, loving, generous Muslims who have become, and will always be, an important part of our lives.'

And so to Gaza

It was in January 2002 that I first met Jonathan. As dawn was breaking on a cold wet day, he arrived in his white van outside the YMCA in West Jerusalem where I was staying. As we shook hands he seemed genuinely pleased that I was interested not only in hearing about the work of his charity, Shevet Achim, but also in being taken to see some of 'his families'.

'Would you like to come to the hospital in Tel Aviv first?' he asked. 'I thought you might like to see the full picture.'

I told him I was in his hands and would be pleased to see all we had time for. And that's when I first noticed this implicit faith he has. 'We're in his hands,' he corrected me, looking up to heaven.

Mind you, when I saw the old, battered white Transit van we were to travel in, I realised faith came into the equation! It obviously had to be coaxed along. But I was impressed by his quiet warmth and sincerity. It was only 7.30 in the morning, but he looked tired, resigned even. He told me he drove to Gaza two, maybe three times a week. Jerusalem to Gaza is a long journey taking two to three hours each way. I sensed that this was a day quite unlike any other for me. I had never been to Gaza before, and to go now in this time of heightened tension and security was forcing me to experience the everyday struggles and frustrations of the people who live in this region of the world.

And so we set off from Jerusalem in the pouring rain.

'The rain usually stops just north of Gaza,' he said. 'If it doesn't, it gets pretty miserable down there.'

I was about to find out.

They are afraid we will kill their babies

The dual carriageway between Jerusalem and Tel Aviv is fast and modern. But in the rush hour it is choked with vehicles and drivers who sound their horns at the slightest annoyance. All this can seem quite nerve-racking if you're not used to driving in such conditions. But

Jonathan took it all in his stride and a couple of rainswept hours later we left the main road and entered the grounds of one of the most sophisticated hospitals in Israel, the Wolfson Medical Centre in Holon, near Tel Aviv.

There we met Dr Houri, head of the Paediatric Centre. This benign, gentle man from Tunisia has dark brown eyes. He had just arrived at the hospital himself, but he seemed delighted to show us around.

'Come and see the Intensive Care Unit.'

As I followed him into the ward, I was struck by how clean and bright it looked. There was a quietness that underlined an intensity of care; teams of medical personnel were working busily around each bed. Toys and brightly coloured pictures were everywhere. Every effort had been made to make this as relaxed an atmosphere as is possible in an intensive care situation.

I could see five or six single beds. On each bed there was what looked like a tiny bundle wrapped in a blanket. We walked up to the first bed, where tubes and monitors surrounded the 'bundle'. On closer inspection I saw a tiny newborn baby with tubes in his arms, in his chest, up his nose, down his throat.

Dr Houri explained that this was a baby from Vietnam. Born with a complex heart problem, he had been brought to the centre through the Save a Child's Heart programme. In fact, Dr Houri explained, fifty per cent of the children they treat in his unit come through this channel.

'I hate refusing any baby that needs an ICU bed,' he told me.

When I asked him why they had so many non-Jewish children from around the world in this hospital he explained that they had developed research links with other hospitals and were involved in training medical personnel from areas where expertise was needed. It was an attitude of wanting to share the knowledge developed at the Wolfson to benefit others. Perhaps that's what happens when you realise that helping other people less fortunate than yourself is a very worthwhile thing to do. Whatever the reason, I was impressed by the attitude of this medical centre and the way it treated as many children as it possibly could.

We moved to the next bed. A similar scene. Beside the bed stood the baby's mother, wrapped in the traditional Muslim dress and headwear; here was a Palestinian baby, from Gaza. Dr Houri explained how this child had been born with a serious heart defect and had required urgent heart surgery. The child had come to the notice of Jonathan Miles, who had contacted Dr Houri, and the doctor had arranged for the operation to be carried out. This child needed three operations; he'd just had the first and, according to Dr Houri, was 'OK'. But he would need to return in a few months' time for the next op, and then again some time in the future.

And would Dr Houri undertake all three operations, I asked.

'Of course,' came the reply without a flicker of hesitation.

'Some of the babies weigh less than a kilo when they come in here,' he told me, 'they are so sick.'

All the time, his eyes were scanning the beds, checking the monitors. At each bed he touched the child, even if just to stroke a foot, as though he was willing them to get better. He seemed to really love each child and, as a doctor, rose to the challenge to save as many lives as he could.

We stopped at the third bed. Here was a girl whom I guessed to be about twelve years old. She had come from Ethiopia. 'She has rheumatic heart disease,' Dr Houri explained. She had needed a replacement valve in her heart.

'Some of the kids that come from Ethiopia arrive here very sick and their hearts are in a bad state. She looks a lot better today than she looked yesterday. She'll be well enough to be moved out of intensive care this afternoon,' he said with a real sense of relief and satisfaction. It was obvious he'd been fighting to save her life. Language may have been a problem between them, but it didn't seem to matter. I spoke to the Ethiopian nurse who was sitting next to the girl and she told me that she regularly accompanied children from Ethiopia to be treated here by Dr Houri.

An Arab mother was tending her baby by the next bed. Jonathan told me how the family had called him a few days previously. The baby needed urgent heart surgery. His doctor in Gaza had called Jonathan, and Jonathan had called Dr Houri. But there was a complication here. The baby was suffering from diarrhoea and couldn't be operated on until this problem was sorted out.

'Thank God we have the treatment to save these babies,' said Dr Houri, 'otherwise this child would have died.'

I asked Jonathan to ask the mother of this child if she was pleased with the treatment her baby was receiving.

'Yes,' he translated, 'they are very kind. I feel peaceful here. The atmosphere is good. I know they are doing all they can to help my baby.'

And, I found out, the hospital looks after the mothers of these children well too. They are given a place to stay, food to eat, a phone card to call home.

Jonathan explained how he sees relationships developing in the hospital between Jewish and Arab mothers. 'They have a lot in common here,' he said. 'If your child is sick and has the same problem as the child in the next bed, you share a common concern and have a point of contact and a reason to talk. It happens automatically.'

To witness this coming together of people who were so afraid of each other in other circumstances was a wonderful and unique experience. I felt I was touching something so precious and so possible. There was no enmity in this hospital ward. All I witnessed was a Jewish medical team trying to save the lives of as many children, many of them Palestinian children from Gaza, as possible. And they were doing it because they really wanted to. The level of care and commitment seemed to be saying, look what is possible when you stop fighting and killing.

'If it wasn't for you, this child would be dead,' I said to Jonathan.

'Here we have the doctors who are willing to help. We hear about the families that need help. We're just happy to be the go-betweens.'

'The Palestinian Authority won't call us direct,' complained Dr Houri. 'If we could get some of these children here quicker, we could save more lives. But they don't trust us. They are afraid we will kill their babies.'

Afraid we will kill their babies . . . these words rang in my ears as we left the Wolfson Medical Centre in Tel Aviv and continued south along the dual carriageway towards Gaza. If that was the opinion that Palestinian people living in Gaza had towards the Jewish medical teams, then what level of hostility was I about to witness? And what or who had given them such an impression? Normally such opinions, when not based on experience, are based on fear, ignorance and misinformation. Dr Salim Munayer (founder and director of the reconciliatory organisation Musalaha) once said to me 'Once you look your "enemy" in the eye, he no longer seems so threatening. And once you start to talk, the enmity starts to melt.' For the Palestinian mothers I had met at the Wolfson Medical Centre, this had been their first trip into Israel; they had never before even met a Jewish person face to face.

It was time to talk to Jonathan. I'd noticed how self-effacing he was in the hospital, as though he was an invisible catalyst involved in a chemical reaction to bring two parties together who would normally have repelled each other. I could see he was totally committed to saving the lives of as many Palestinian children as he could; there was nothing else on his agenda.

'God prepared good works,' he said. 'We just have to be faithful in understanding him.'

So that was it. He felt he was just playing out the role God had already prepared for him to do. Was that how he managed to remain so calm and unflustered? Did he really believe that it was God who was making it possible for him to defy the political odds in bringing these babies out of the Gaza Strip even in these times of increased unrest and clampdown?

But, I was thinking, it's one thing doing humanitarian aid work; it's another thing really developing a love for and interest in the people you are helping. Where did his love for these people come from?

'If our hearts hadn't been changed by the Lord . . .' he went on.

'We have hopes but not plans. We pray we can expand the model we've developed in Gaza to the rest of the Middle East.'

And the chances of that happening in the present unrest?

'I am thankful to see the bridge has been able to stay open; many others have closed.' He was choosing his words carefully.

'There's been pressure to burn this particular bridge by
parties in Gaza who favour incitement and division,
whether in the name of nationalism or religion; people
who don't want to see people brought closer together
right now. On a practical level, I see religion dividing people; Arabs feeling they have been rejected by God when
they hear talk about the Jews being the only people chosen by God. It's surprising how often I hear that theme
coming up. I believe reconciliation between people is a
spiritual issue, so the good news about Jesus, to those of
us who aren't Jews, is that he has brought those of us who
are afar back to himself. This approach takes us right back
to the biblical roots of the conflict. If the children of
Abraham who were put out of the camp can be brought
back in, that's a healing message, and through Jesus reconciliation and restoration are possible.'

I was impressed by how simply yet profoundly he
understood the situation. Here was a man who believed
the claims of the Bible and, in his own small way, was
trying to put this theory into practice. Could it be that
the ripple effect he was creating was in fact capable of
changing the spiritual climate of families, then spreading into communities and eventually into the nation and
thereby bringing about a change in the political situation? As we drove south, I found myself talking to a man
who believed implicitly that this was the case. Here was
a living example of how one man had gradually
explored an opportunity that he believed God had given
him to effect change in the lives of one family followed
by another and another and then another. With each success, Jonathan's faith had grown, and then his vision had
grown. Now he believed that this reconciliatory work
that God had given him to do was not only saving the
lives of the babies involved but bringing about a lasting

understanding and peace between Jewish and Arab people as well.

I was soon to visit the homes of Muslim families who owed the lives of their children to one American Christian who was putting what he believed possible to the ultimate test. Would I hear these families denouncing terrorism, preferring instead to find a peaceful way of bringing about a just and lasting peace between Arabs and Jews? It occurred to me also that if there were people in Gaza opposed to Jonathan's work, people who didn't want to encourage peacemaking at this particular point in time, I was embarking on a dangerous mission.

'It's hell down there'

I'd never been to Gaza before, yet thought I knew what to expect, having watched television reports during the recent troubles. Strange how watching images on television can make you feel you know a place. And in a sense that is true. But can pictures express the full horror of what it's like to live there? I was about to smell the earth and meet the gaze of those who live in one of the most densely populated areas on the face of the earth, and enter their world, if only for a few brief hours.

With the checkpoint in sight, Jonathan explained that normally the car park would be full of people leaving and entering Gaza. Thousands of people poured out of Gaza to work in Tel Aviv and neighbouring towns every day, only to return en masse each evening. But not now. The border was closed and nobody could go to work. The car park seemed huge, and gave me an idea of the activity that is possible here in quieter times. Because of the security situation, we couldn't even drive the van through to Gaza but had to park it on the Israeli side and cross the border on foot. So, carrying boxes of medicines, we reported to Passport Control on the Israeli side of the Eretz crossing. The young Israeli soldier joked with us. He wanted to know what we could tell him about Samuel Beckett. Why Samuel Beckett? Apparently he was studying English and had an essay to write about Samuel Beckett!

As he checked our passports he wondered why we wanted to go to 'that place', jerking his head in the direction of Gaza. 'It's hell down there,' he said.

How did he know? Had he been there or just watched the TV pictures the same as me?

Jonathan Miles seemed impervious to the banter. This softly spoken American's quiet determination mixed with resignation was even more apparent in this situation. He seemed careful to keep his opinions to himself. And so I listened as he joked back with the young Israeli soldier in Hebrew.

'What are you doing here again?' the soldier asked him in English. 'You come down here a lot. Delivering more medicine?'

'Yes,' replied Jonathan, as he proceeded to comply with the necessary bureaucracy. He chatted further with the young soldier and asked him how he was finding it working here on the border.

'It's boring here,' came the reply. Better to be boring and peaceful. I thought.

Formalities and paperwork complete, we left the passport office and walked towards the Israeli checkpoint. It was cold and pouring with rain. The rain hadn't stopped north of Gaza after all.

Jonathan didn't seem in a hurry. He took time to chat with the Israeli soldiers at the first checkpoint. He enquired how they were and exchanged words about the weather. Israelis are not much used to rain, although they were grateful for it, as the country had been suffering from a severe drought. They seemed pleased to talk, indeed pleased to see somebody because the checkpoint was quiet. With the recent outbreak of terrorism and suicide bombers, the Israelis had secured the checkpoint. It was eerily quiet and the atmosphere felt nervous. These soldiers, men and women in their late teens and early twenties, were on duty in one of the tensest places on earth. Standing guard on a border where there was hardly a soul to be seen, in bleak surroundings on a grey, cold, wet winter's day; surrounded by cameras and fully armed, they were, after all, only doing their job in a dangerous and volatile situation. I didn't envy them one bit.

And so we turned our backs on Israel and walked towards Gaza. It reminded me of films I'd seen set in the Cold War. Checkpoints between east and west during the communist era. Soldiers at either end. Watchtowers. Suspicion. Tension. Everybody's nerves taught. The slightest wrong move and guns would fire. I followed Jonathan. This was a routine trip for him; driving from his home in Jerusalem, parking his old white van in the large car park on the Israeli side, only to use another old van parked on the Palestinian side.

We proceeded to walk through the checkpoint towards the Palestinian border post. The walls are high. The barbed wire ominous. The road is blocked to prevent anybody from trying to force their way through in a vehicle. The walk seemed long and lonely. The suspicion and fear were tangible. Do Jews and Palestinians hate each other this much? Or is this to prevent the crazy few from blighting the situation for both communities, depriving ordinary peace-loving people of the opportunity to go to work, provide for their children and live a peaceful existence? It seemed unreal. I tried to imagine what it would be like travelling through this checkpoint every day to go to work. What does it do to the mind, being treated as a potential terrorist or believing that everybody is a potential terrorist? The hunter and the hunted: who is who? How easy it is for a few people to wreak havoc for the majority.

Jonathan was unfazed. Carrying two large boxes of medical supplies, he chatted amicably with the Palestinian soldiers in Arabic. He speaks the language fluently as a result of his six years living in Gaza. And the interesting thing was, he seemed to be genuinely pleased to be there. There was no hint that this was a job that had to be got out of the way as quickly as possible. He seemed to bring sanity to an insane situation. He was being a light in a dark place, bringing some cheer where there was only misery. I was already seeing that one person can do a lot to change the situation for good. Even taking the time to stand and chat for a few minutes and exchange a few kind words made such a difference to the lives of the young Israeli soldiers as well as these Palestinian soldiers. Same man, same message; received well by both sides. I wondered if Jonathan's apparent impartiality was the key. But I think why he is so well received is because he genuinely takes an interest in everybody he meets and treats them with equal respect.

On reaching the 'other' side we walked up to a white van parked at the back of some sheds. Jonathan took the keys from his pocket, unlocked the van and carefully placed the boxes of medicine on the back seat. He told me he'd had trouble starting the engine the previous time and now, sure enough, after several days of endless rain, the battery was totally flat. The engine would not start.

A few Palestinian soldiers came over to help. They seemed to like Jonathan and wanted to help. A committee was quickly formed and they enthusiastically offered a number of solutions as to how the van could be started. Eventually, after long negotiations, they arranged themselves behind the van, and whilst Jonathan attempted to steer it over the rough ground strewn with rocks and debris, they started to push. An elderly Palestinian taxi driver joined the troop and tried his hardest, but his wheezing chest could be heard by all, and with an asthma attack imminent, he retired to his well-used, shabby, yellow Mercedes taxi that seemed to rattle as much as he did.

I had the impression that these Palestinian soldiers didn't really feel comfortable with my assistance in pushing the van. So I withdrew and used the time to look casually around. Just inside the tall perimeter fence, ripe oranges and grapefruits hung heavily on the branches of citrus trees. These trees reached up the road as far as the eye could see. In fact, there was so much fruit ripening that it was starting to fall off and the ground was littered with fruit – it seemed such a waste when there were reports that people here were hungry. Then along came an elderly woman riding on top of a cart laden with what looked like coriander, pulled by a tired-looking donkey. She was sat astride her 'harvest'. What was she going to do with such a quantity of coriander, I wondered. I suddenly felt propelled back in time. An hour earlier I'd been at the Wolfson Medical Centre in Tel Aviv, seeing some of the most sophisticated life-support equipment in the world. And here was an old woman riding on a rickety wooden cart pulled by a donkey!

Even further along the road, goats and sheep were wandering in and out of the orange groves; their colours ranged from cream through to brown, with some speckled. The goats had long ears, as did some of the sheep – from a distance it was hard to tell them apart. The entire flock seemed to be limping. It was only when I got closer that I noticed their front legs were tied with rope, giving them little scope to wander far. Looking more closely, I could see the rope was cutting into their legs; they were hobbling and looked in real pain. I felt a pang of horror at this appalling display of cruelty. Is life that cheap here? What sort of a person ties the legs of his animals together – somebody who has little regard for inflicting pain on helpless animals? Was this one example of brutality an indication of a deep current of anger and resentment? A chilling feeling went through me. What else was I to witness today?

My attention was drawn back to the activity surrounding the van. Finally, after several strenuous attempts at pushing it backwards and forwards, the engine reluctantly started. Jonathan drove it around the compound a couple of times just to warm it up a little, then it was time to head south to Gaza City. As we drove along the bumpy, potholed road, I noticed many of the buildings looked only half built. Some of the houses were designed on a grand scale with potential for balconies and the traditional Arab arched windows and doorways. But times were hard and buildings were in poor repair. I was told that there are currently more people living in Gaza per square mile than in Bangladesh.

We passed hens and dogs, cats and sheep, children, men on bicycles, women balancing large baskets on their heads, battered yellow taxis with toothless drivers wearing caps or scarves round their heads to keep out the cold. Familiar yet strange sights everywhere I looked. A visual cacophony of discordant, disjointed life. So many men on the streets; unable to go to work, they had nothing to do – yet there was so much to do. So much rubbish to clear. So many roads to mend. So many broken cars. Unfinished houses. Broken telephone wires. Fruit falling off the trees.

We were on our way to visit the Tatar family. Abdul Rahim was born with a serious heart defect and recently Jonathan had organised for him to have surgery at the Wolfson Medical Centre. We drove for an hour and eventually arrived in Gaza City. The family live in an apartment in a five-storey building. With few signposts, and even fewer street signs, Jonathan had to ask his way. Eventually we arrived outside a tall building. A large iron door painted a bright shade of blue was half open. Jonathan checked with some children who had gathered excitedly around the van that this was where the Tatar family lived, and after climbing the dark, unlit, unfinished concrete stairwell, we entered their apartment.

I was surprised to be in a room with bright white walls. A bright red rug covered the floor in stark contrast to the walls. Around the edge of the room, white plastic patio chairs were arranged, and in the centre a white oval plastic table was covered by a white cloth. A tall vase full of red plastic roses stood erect in the centre of the table, and clusters of bright yellow plastic roses were suspended from the ceiling in the corners of the room. Everything was bright, very bright.

Apparently Jamil, the father, had once been a metalworker in Israel, crossing from Gaza at the Eretz crossing every day. Times then were good. He'd started to build this new home to provide enough space for his immediate family, as well as his married sons and their wives. But the *intifada* put an end to that. With the border crossing closed, Jamil hadn't been able to go to work in Israel for over a year – and no work means no income. The house remained unfinished, and if it were not for the eldest son still working in Gaza itself, we were told, there would be no money coming into the family. Their eldest son earned 600 shekels a month, the equivalent of £100. With the price of food high, Jamil complained, the money was soon spent. But despite their dire circumstances and ten children to feed, Abdul's mother, Suad, struck me as a strong, defiant woman who kept a scrupulously clean and tidy home. This family had clearly known better times and was trying to maintain a dignified lifestyle and make the best of its reduced circumstances.

After the children had been introduced and we'd all shaken hands, and Abdul's condition had been discussed, we were served hot, sweet Arabic coffee with chicory. It's an acquired taste. I happen to like it! Jonathan spoke with them in fluent Arabic. They called him Abu George – father of George – because his eldest son is called George. I noticed they treated him with genuine affection and respect, perhaps because he's lived amongst these people. They were honoured that he had returned to visit them; touched that he was taking an interest in their situation. He was prepared to sit and listen, unhurried, and so a torrent of conversation flowed out of Suad in particular. She was unstoppable. Here was somebody willing to sit quietly and sympathise with her difficulties. But also, it seemed to me, they appreciated Jonathan because he had made a difference to their lives. He did, after all, save the life of their son. There's nobody else in Gaza who has the clout or the contacts to arrange urgent heart surgery for Palestinian children in Israeli hospitals. He'd clearly earned their respect. Does it take six years living in Gaza to reach this level of acceptance? What a costly investment.

We listened to the story of Abdul's recovery and drank more coffee. We had other families to visit. I waited for Jonathan to make the first move. I felt sure he'd stand up and make our farewells soon. But he remained seated on his white plastic chair. I noticed various children in the family put their heads shyly around the door to look at us. Their large brown eyes stared at us, intrigued. Considering there were so many children in the family, there was no noise, no shouting, just quiet. I looked back into their eyes. I couldn't speak their language but I could meet their gaze. Abdul seemed afraid to come any closer. Apparently he thought I was a doctor and, after so many visits to see various specialists, he'd become terrified of anybody who might be vaguely medical. We soon put his mind at rest. These young children seemed strangely old for their age. Perhaps it was because their brother had just recovered from his operation, having so nearly lost his life. Or perhaps it was because of the *intifada*; their father at home, unable to go to work; overhearing their parents discussing how they were going to manage, or the talk on the street with other children about what they were going to do with their lives. What does your future look like when your only link with the outside world is Palestinian Authority TV with its anti-Israel rhetoric and incitement to hate and fight?

What was happening? Suad moved the red roses from the centre of the table and took away the coffee cups. Then she returned from the kitchen with an extremely large circular tray. I could hardly believe my eyes. On the tray were two roasted chickens, each split in half and filled with rice and cashew nuts. Hummus sprinkled with chickpeas and parsley was spread on two paper plates. We were each given a yellow plastic plate and a basket full of freshly baked pitta bread was passed round. Suad laughed at our surprise. Ripping off a large piece of chicken with her fingers, she pushed it into my mouth. 'Eat, eat,' she seemed to be saying.

Jamil, Abdul's father, sat quietly. Dressed in a traditional long blue Arab shirt, with an anorak to keep him warm against the cold (although he was barefooted), he explained why he wasn't eating. He was suffering with diabetes and high blood pressure. I tried to guess his age: probably not yet 50, but he looked about 65. His teeth, or those remaining, were yellow. He wore dark glasses. His forehead was deeply furrowed. He tried to put on a brave face, but you could see that the frustration of not being able to work to provide for his children and finish building his house, not to mention putting enough food on the table to feed his large family, was taking a toll on his health.

His gratitude to Jonathan for the help he had given them in organising treatment for Abdul at the medical centre in Tel Aviv made him emotional.

Again and again, he kept repeating his appreciation to Jonathan and his thanks to Allah for the gift of Abdul. It was touching to witness this raw display of heartfelt gratitude from a proud man who was desperately trying to maintain his dignity.

I wondered how Suad had felt about leaving Gaza with Abdul and spending time with him in an Israeli hospital. It was the first time she had been to Israel, and television pictures and talk on the street had made her believe that all Israelis were aggressors. Had she been afraid?

'At first, yes,' she admitted. But her fears had been quickly put to rest. She described how kind the Israeli medical team had been to her. How they had made sure she had all she needed – food, accommodation and information about her son's condition. She had been touched by the care and attention shown to her by Israeli mothers whose children, too, were being treated for serious heart problems. Their shared experience seemed to give them a common ground for concern that had nothing to do with the conflict raging between the two communities.

It seemed Suad had had her prejudices about Israelis well and truly turned around. Jamil was not slow in describing his frustration towards Arafat. 'Arafat doesn't care about us,' he continued. 'We hear about donations of money from other Arab countries, but we don't benefit. Where does this money go?' He put his hand behind him to indicate how be believed Arafat's advisors must be pocketing the money themselves.

'Is this a widely held view amongst people here?' I ventured to ask. It seemed dangerous talk.

'Yes,' came the reply, 'we cannot survive another year like this.'

It left me wondering whether a few more months of this *intifada* would see Arafat unseated by his own people.

Eventually, and a few cups of coffee later, we left Abdul and his family, but not before Suad had produced a tin of toffees and insisted I fill my handbag with them for my children. I felt guilty at taking what little she had. Wondering what I should do, I looked at Jonathan for advice. 'Just accept them,' he said quietly. 'It's the only way Suad can express her thanks for Abdul.'

'*Shukran*, Suad,' I said, trying to sound grateful, 'thank you.'

Once out in the street, we were surrounded by bright-eyed Palestinian children. They came up close and pressed against us, obviously wondering what we were doing: the toffees came in useful! Dirty hands eagerly plucked the brightly wrapped sweets from my hand and delighted smiles and laughter erupted from their grubby faces. I suppose when you have nothing, a toffee makes a difference to your day.

It was fortunate that we had parked the van on a hill, because the battery still refused to start the engine. So Jonathan gently released the handbrake and allowed the van to coast downhill before putting it into gear and jump-starting the engine into life. Leaving Gaza City we journeyed further south for another hour. It was mid-afternoon and still raining heavily.

This will take a long time

There were people everywhere. Donkeys pulling carts. Children playing barefoot in the streets. Half-built houses of grey breeze-block. Satellite dishes perched precariously on roofs. Traders. Oranges. Grapefruits. Lemons. The land is fertile. The soil rich and generous in the food it yields.

We passed the Neztarium Crossing where a Palestinian boy had died in his father's arms, caught in crossfire between Palestinian and Israeli soldiers. These crossings, heavily guarded to protect the Jewish settlers as they are bussed through, have become the focus of the struggle in Gaza. The buildings all around have been flattened by Israeli tanks to guard against snipers. The remaining neighbouring buildings, riddled with bullet holes, are now deserted by their occupants. I was witnessing a level of distrust and defensive action that has to be seen to be believed. Guns. Tanks. It was all here. Both sides equally frightened of each other. All with mothers, sisters, fathers, brothers, anxiously hoping to see their young men again soon, alive.

Round the next bend, the traffic slowed to a grinding halt. An Israeli tank had left the road and become stuck in deep mud. Another tank was attempting to pull it out. The soldiers looked nervous as they worked with guns in hand, waving and gesticulating to each other, some giving orders, others trying to carry them out.

We inched past. We'd be back later to see whether the rescue mission had been successful.

A few minutes later, the traffic came to a standstill once again. 'This will take a long time,' said Jonathan, reluctant to switch off the engine in case it would not start again. Now it was raining hard and the thought of having to push the van worried him.

In the distance I could see a crossroads. Once again the buildings all around had been demolished. On one side of the road was an Israeli watchtower. I could see the heavily armed soldiers guarding the road and looking through binoculars into the distance. After a few minutes a column of vehicles approached the crossing. Armoured trucks led the way, followed by three coaches full of people, and more armoured trucks brought up the rear. 'Settlers,' said Jonathan. His voice betrayed no emotion. I couldn't tell whether or not he approved. But I wondered what made these people so determined to live where they did, under guard, under siege, amongst a people who preferred them not to be there, some of whom wished them dead.

Then, as though a train had passed through the level crossing, the barriers were lifted and we were on our way again. It was raining so hard and the roads were so wet that at times they seemed to merge with the surrounding fields. In the towns, the roads resembled waterfalls; cascades of water flowed through the streets, filling potholes, meandering around people's legs. We passed bedraggled, hungry-looking donkeys pulling wooden carts laden with people or oranges. Cars and buses, driving through vast puddles, splashed people on the pavements who were sheltering as best they could in the dilapidated doorways and under vendors' stalls.

Minutes later, as it was starting to get dark, Jonathan stopped the van in a narrow street. On one side there were houses and on the other a brick wall that it was just possible to see over. We were close to the sea. On the other side of the wall, surrounded by sand dunes, were two tall blocks of flats reaching into the sky – Jonathan casually nodded his head in their direction and explained they were homes of Israeli settlers; the same people we had seen speeding through the checkpoint in coaches just a few minutes earlier.

I looked at the close proximity of these flats to their Arab 'neighbours'. There was something so incongruous about it. Living so near to each other, yet never meeting. Watching each other's every move, yet never speaking. So near, yet so far. I wondered what effect it has on both communities living under siege like this for so long, with no apparent end to hostilities in sight.

The moment I stepped out of the van, a group of curious children gathered; they seemed to appear from nowhere. I remembered the toffees Suad had forced on me earlier in the day, and reached in my bag to draw some out. The children pressed in closer. It was raining and the light was fading fast. There are few street lights in this part of the world. As I drew out a handful of sweets, the children laughed with delight and eagerly took them. Children who had held back out of shyness now seemed suddenly interested in what was on offer, and in no time at all, the vast quantity of toffees that Suad had given me earlier had disappeared.

Jonathan, having parked the van and ascertained which door we were to go through, led the way. He was carrying two boxes of medicine. I followed him through the iron door into a corridor. It was dark and we had to feel our way at first, as our eyes grew accustomed to the dimness. The dark damp stairwell up to the Salams' apartment was cold and grey. The concrete building blocks unfinished. The steps rough. We climbed four flights of stairs. On the way, each apartment we passed was unfinished, doorways and windows gaping holes like empty eye sockets through which the rain and wind blew relentlessly.

At the top, a door opened into an apartment, the home of the Salam family. Abdul Salam Abu Said greeted us and beside him his wife, Halima Um Said, stood holding her baby. An intelligent-looking woman, she wore glasses and looked studious. Other children gathered around her, including two girls aged between 10 and 12. They bore a remarkable resemblance to their mother; or was it that they all wore the same style of glasses? On finding out I was English, Halima said a very tentative 'Hello'.

'Do you speak English?' I asked.

'No, no!' Halima laughed. But I could tell she did!

Inside the apartment, their home was bright and clean and orderly. A stark contrast to the dark, unfinished staircase we had just climbed.

Halima gave me her baby, Abdul, to hold. He was coughing and his chest sounded wheezy. Only two months old, Abdul had been born with a serious heart condition which had required urgent surgery. At five days old, his life had hung in the balance. I later learnt that the family had already lost one baby in similar circumstances. But on this occasion, they had managed to contact Jonathan and he had arranged the operation. Now Abdul was making good progress, although he still needed drugs, which Jonathan was now delivering to the family.

As I held Abdul I prayed he would get better. He looked so tiny. At first he lay peacefully in my arms, quite

content to be held by a complete stranger. But it didn't
last. It started when his fingers started to move, then his
arms, then I felt his body moving as though he was
stretching himself. It was all going badly wrong! He started to cry, so I stood up and started walking around the
room with him. Halima was nowhere in sight. She had
disappeared behind a curtain to make some tea. Her
daughters started to giggle. They seemed to find it very
amusing that I had been given their baby brother to hold,
and doubtless were wondering quite how I was going to
comfort him. One of them ran off and came back with a
dummy, but that didn't work.

I lifted him higher onto my shoulder, all the time con-
scious that he had had open-heart surgery a few days
previously. Was he in pain from the scar, I wondered? I
felt as though I was handling a piece of delicate porcelain
china, liable to break at any time. But as long as I kept
moving, Abdul kept quiet. That seemed a good arrange-
ment, and his sisters appeared to approve. His eyes followed the bright colours of the pictures on the wall and
the plastic flowers that hung from some bookshelves. I
noticed a photograph of Jonathan taken at the Wolfson –
he was surrounded by parents holding their babies, and
Dr Houri was in the picture too. Abdul's eyelids began to
close. Perhaps he would go to sleep.

More people started to arrive. Wet through from the
rain, they were apparently friends and relatives of
the family. They had heard Jonathan was visiting and
wanted to come and meet him. Halima's father was one
of the first to arrive. Dressed in a traditional long dark
grey Arab shirt and with a little white hat on his head, he
came and shook my hand, the expression on his face
breaking into a broad smile when he saw me holding the
baby. I felt like the au pair!

More and more people squeezed into the room. It quickly became very overcrowded. A man pushed his way across the room to talk to Jonathan. His teenage daughter, Hilean, had undergone heart surgery at the hospital in Gaza a year ago, but it had not been successful. Could Jonathan arrange for her to see the doctor at the Wolfson Centre? I looked at his daughter. She was shy and looked embarrassed, her face partly hidden behind her scarf. Her father, Abed, Jonathan explained, was a mathematics teacher at the United Nations School in Gaza; Hilean, he said, was constantly tired and her health was deteriorating.

As I continued to rock Abdul in my arms and walk around the increasingly crowded room, glasses of sweet mint tea and a plate of cakes were produced. The door opened again, and a mother entered the room with her nine-year-old son and made straight for the settee where Jonathan was sitting reading the medical notes of Hilean.

His attention was drawn away when he saw the boy. Apparently he lived in a nearby refugee camp. His name was Yusef Asmar. He was born with a small hole in his heart and his mother was concerned about his health, so she had come to ask Jonathan to arrange for him to see a doctor.

Patiently Jonathan sat and quietly and calmly talked to the family in Arabic. He was in no hurry. By this time the room was full of people. It was very dark outside and the rain was lashing down.

The Jewish doctors will kill your baby

It was then Halima told me her story. I asked her how she had felt about going with her baby to Israel for medical attention. She told me that she had never been to Israel before and was very, very afraid to go. People had told her the Israelis would kill her child. She was frightened. But what could she do? If she didn't go, her baby would die in any case. She had already lost one child. For a moment, her face looked sad as the memory of having to make that difficult decision raced back.

'I knew my baby was dying. But there was nothing the medical team at the hospital in Gaza could do to save him. Our only hope was to take him to a hospital in Israel. But they were telling me not to go to Israel. I looked at my baby. He was only a few hours old but I knew something was terribly wrong. He was blue all over. He looked dreadfully ill. It was all so familiar. I had lost a baby in this way before. I couldn't bear to lose this little boy as well.

'What should I do? The clock was ticking. Life was ebbing away from my baby. I looked at my husband. I thought of our other children. I looked at my baby boy. I had to find a way of saving his life. I was in a dilemma. "Don't go," some of my family told me. "The Jewish doctors will kill your baby. Don't you know all Jews hate Palestinians?" I felt under such pressure. I wanted my baby to live. If I didn't go, my baby would die in any case. I was very, very nervous. I had never been to Israel. I had never left Gaza. I didn't know what to expect in Israel. I had never spoken to a Jewish person. I didn't know a word of Hebrew. I had to decide to watch my baby die or risk taking him to the hospital in Tel Aviv.'

To Halima, Israel could have been on another planet, it was so far removed from her experience of life. Her only knowledge of Israel was what she had seen on Palestinian Authority television. Her perception was one-sided. Maybe the border with Israel was only an hour's drive away, but to Halima, Israel was another world – a world of danger and mistrust; a world she would ordinarily never contemplate visiting. But this was no ordinary situation.

'We had heard of Jonathan Miles. I knew he had lived in Gaza with his family for several years, and that he arranged for Palestinian children with serious heart conditions to be seen by doctors at the Wolfson Medical Centre in Tel Aviv. I'd heard reports about other babies who had been there for surgery and survived and returned safely to their families in Gaza. And this helped me to make up my mind. So, in desperation we telephoned Jonathan and asked him to help us. And very quickly he arranged for our baby to be taken to Israel for surgery. Jonathan told me I had nothing to fear. So I put my trust in him, and in God, and leaving my husband and five children behind, went with my baby to Tel Aviv.'

Then she laughed. Perhaps because she had just had one of the most extraordinary experiences that any human being can undergo. She entrusted her own life and the life of her newborn baby into the hands of the 'enemy' – and lived to tell the tale: an experience that has changed her outlook on life, and the lives of those around her.

'So what happened?' I asked her.

Halima described how ecstatic she had been about the treatment she received. The doctors, she told me, were so kind. They immediately put her mind at rest. They told her exactly what was wrong with Abdul and how they intended to correct the problem in the operating theatre. She met Israeli mothers whose children had the same problem. She made friends there. She told me that she now knows Israelis are not bad people who hate Palestinians. They too want peace and an end to violence. She told me how she had told her friends and family about her experience.

A few steps to the left, then a few to the right

As I watched Jonathan, surrounded as he was by a queue
of anxious parents concerned for their children's health, I
wondered was this the result of one man taking his wife
and children to go and live in Gaza for a few years, sending his children to the local school where they learnt to
speak perfect Arabic? Building and nurturing the trust
and respect of the Muslim community there and being
prepared to act as a go-between, the catalyst between
Palestinian family and Israeli doctor to save the lives of
children born with life-threatening heart problems? Was I
witnessing how one man was directly affecting a change
in attitude in hundreds of families, and indirectly in the
lives of thousands? Is Jonathan doing something that no
politician is able to do? Are his actions changing the political climate in Gaza and proving to ordinary people there
that Jewish people do not want to kill Palestinians; that
there are many kind and peace-loving Israelis who are
desperate to see the checkpoints and barbed wire dis-
mantled?

We left – eventually. I handed Abdul back to his
mother – still awake. Then began the journey back to
Jerusalem. We had spent at least three hours driving
south from the Eretz crossing. It was pitch dark outside.
The van wouldn't start and had to be pushed before it
stubbornly spluttered into life. We swung out of the narrow street and into the main thoroughfare once again and
passed the place where the Israeli tank had earlier been
stuck in the mud. There was nothing there now, so we
assumed it had been successfully pulled out. Beyond the
town, the road was unlit. The rain poured down, and
road and field merged into one glutinous, dark quagmire.
Jonathan didn't seem worried. He steadily drove along

and somehow we stayed on the road. He started to make some calls on his mobile phone. He explained he was arranging for Hilean and Yusef to see a specialist at the Wolfson. His phone rang. Another sick baby urgently needed attention. More calls to the Wolfson. Backwards and forwards the conversations continued, sometimes in Arabic, sometimes in Hebrew.

There was a sense of urgency: every effort had to be made to help these children. Perhaps he was afraid the border would soon be closed and then it would be impossible to bring these children out.

I sat in the back of the van, watching as the traffic moving in the opposite direction twisted and skewed around on the wet and muddy road.

Are we given windows of opportunity that one day may suddenly be closed, I wondered?

After a couple of hours we arrived back at the Eretz crossing and parked the van in its usual place behind the sheds. The strong searchlights illuminated our walk back through the checkpoint. Through the narrow crack in the bunker, we showed our passports to the Palestinian soldiers then began the long walk through the obstacles towards the Israeli side. A few steps to the left, then a few to the right, our way dictated by blocks of concrete. We re-entered the Passport Control office to have our documents scrutinised once again. I looked for the Israeli soldier who had asked about Samuel Beckett. But he'd gone. There was no one to joke with us this time. All was quiet, routine even.

We walked to the empty car park where the van was parked. I imagined once again what it must be like when thirty thousand pour out of Gaza to go to work in Israel every day. How the car park must be full of buses and cars then. Chaos! But here, today, nothing, nobody. Emptiness. Sorrow.

But I had memories that would remain. A story that is true. I had spoken to all concerned. I had seen with my own eyes the miracle of reconciliation and what one person can do to make a difference. One American Christian standing in the middle between Jew and Arab, saving lives; changing attitudes; building a climate of peace that the majority of people yearn for.

To contact Jonathan Miles, Coordinator, Shevet Achim: www.shevet.org
'Behold how good and how pleasant for brothers to dwell together in unity' Psalm 133.

Jerusalem office: PO Box 32296, Jerusalem 91000, Israel
Office managers: Phil and Martha Berg, bergs@shevet.org

US office for tax-deductible receipts: PO Box 1006, Rocky Face, GA 30740, USA.
Office manager: Donna Petrel, donna@shevet.org

UK contributions payable to CFI at: CFI Communications, PO Box 2687, Eastbourne, E. Sussex, BN22 7LZ, UK.
Tel 01323 410810
info@cfi.org.uk

CHAPTER 3

FROM LILLE TO JERUSALEM

'You have to be on one side or the other. You can't believe in reconciliation in the Holy Land – it's impossible.'

So said my Muslim Palestinian friend. Born in the Old City of Jerusalem over forty years ago, educated in a Catholic school there, now married to a Catholic English girl and living in the UK. That was his perspective.

'You're wasting your time trying to bring the two sides together,' he argued.

'But,' I wanted to tell him, 'I know it's happening, I've seen it with my own eyes.'

What follows is the true story of how a French Catholic nun, a German Protestant, a former Orthodox now Messianic Jewish believer and an Arab Christian came to meet in Jerusalem. It would be fair to say it's a bizarre story and one that is still in the process of being lived out. They believe their destiny is linked to the future return of Jesus and the preparation of the church to be ready, like a bride, for the bridegroom's arrival.

Their paths crossed in Jerusalem only a few years ago but their individual journeys to Jerusalem from different parts of the world began long before that. Today they meet regularly to pray and study the Bible together to discover what God's destiny is for Israel and for the Jews and

Palestinians who live there. Reconciliation is at the core of their belief, reconciliation between God and man and between Jew and Gentile. They share a common belief in the death and resurrection of Jesus, and in his promise to return to Jerusalem in glory (as referred to in Acts 1).

In case you are thinking this is the stuff of make-believe, some strange idealism born out of a naive idea that ancient feuds and more modern injustices can be forgotten in a moment to enable a surreal coming together of these hitherto shattered relationships, then let me try to persuade you otherwise by telling you what I witnessed during 2002 in Jerusalem, two years into a bloody war (others call it an *intifada*) that shows no sign of abating.

It was almost by chance that I first met Marie Yeshua in January 2002. She is a sister in the monastery of Poor Clare, situated behind high walls in the Talpiot district of Jerusalem. Marie Yeshua's journey to Jerusalem started just over twenty years ago when she decided as a young woman to walk from the community in Nice, where she was living at the time, to Jerusalem. She set off by herself on a pilgrimage that took her several months across Europe via Rome to Jerusalem.

The day we first met was cold and wet; just a couple of days after I had travelled into Gaza with Jonathan Miles. Winter days in Jerusalem can be bitter and this was no exception. The imposing, heavy wooden door into the monastery was as tall as the bare stone walls that surround it. The taxi driver who dropped me off cast a nervous glance over his shoulder as he drove off, doubtless wondering if anybody lived on the other side of such a forbidding wall. I felt as though I was standing on the outside of a prison waiting to be let in. I had absolutely no idea what to expect, but when the door swung open I found myself in a rather overgrown but very attractive garden. The trees were dripping water and the stone pathway cradled puddles.

As I walked up the drive, it was like stepping back in time. The monastery had a tired and slightly impoverished look to it. But on the step to welcome us (I had been taken to meet Marie by my friend Dr Petra Heldt, a theologian originally from Germany, now director of the Theological Research Fraternity in Jerusalem) was Marie Yeshua. I was immediately struck by her. She looked tall and very slender, an impression perhaps exaggerated by the shapeless brown habit she was wearing. She spoke excitedly in her broken English and we laughed about the weather: she laughs a lot!

'Come on in out of the rain,' she said in her heavy French accent. 'Let me make you some tea.' And with that she disappeared off down a long corridor and left us in a large room. Although only early afternoon, it was dark inside the monastery. In the centre of the room was a long wooden table – the sort you would expect to see in a monastery – surrounded by plain wooden chairs. The walls were the colour of parchment with an occasional icon to break the monotony. It was sparse. And the silence – there was such a hush in the place, I could almost hear myself breathing.

Marie Yeshua returned with the tea, and we were joined by one of her friends who had offered to help with the translation; since she was fluent in French and English her help was invaluable.

The story started to unfold. What was Marie doing here?

Sister Marie Yeshua

'It's a long story. I didn't make the decision to travel from Nice to Jerusalem. I believe it had to do with being aware of and listening to the voice of Providence. Far ahead of us, God knows what is best for us, and what our choices should be.

'When I was a teenager I was passionate about discovering the meaning of life – not God, that came later. It was an adolescent crisis. My mother realised that I was serious about this search (I later understood that she was following me at a distance), but she knew she did not have the answers to my questions. So one day, in desperation, she said to me "There's a monastery up the road; go and speak to those women, maybe they have the answers for you."

'It was a monastery of Poor Clares. The sister I met was a young woman of about 30, Sister Marie Pierre. Hers was a powerful story. She had once been a model and two or three years after her conversion she entered the monastery: talk about a change of lifestyle! I used to visit her twice a month for at least a couple of hours, so I had a great deal of conversation with her on many subjects. At the end of two or three years of meeting her she told me "You have a vocation." But I refused to believe her and I left and never went back!

'I started to study interior design although I knew that was not what I wanted to do with my life. So, before long, I left home and after two or three years of moving from place to place I arrived at a community called Berdine, a Christian community that exists to welcome marginalized people – former prisoners, drug addicts and alcoholics. In those days I believed that the fundamental question of life was "Why is there suffering?" And for me Berdine provided an answer, because it was a reservoir of the poorest among God's people. I was able to experiment through prayer and I discovered that it was possible to touch something in a person that had been destroyed, something which humanly speaking could not be expected to change or improve.

'The founder of the Berdine community, Henri Catta, and several of its members began to ask themselves why, two thousand years after the Good News, the world was still in a state of sin and suffering. The only answer we received was: because the Christian world is so disunited; it is a counter-testimony. The community was always very open to ecumenicism, and we were introduced to Thomas Roberts, a pastor and prophet. He taught that there will never be unity in the church until it repents towards its "older brother", the Jews, who are "the roots of the church". I became very intrigued by his ideas and felt my spirit rising to the challenge. So when he announced that he was organising a pilgrimage to Jerusalem in 1984, I took the decision to go. It sounded important to me for Protestants, Orthodox and Catholics to jointly make a pilgrimage to Jerusalem to meet the "older brother" and to take part in acts of repentance. In fact, I took it so seriously that I decided to walk to Jerusalem from France.

'I travelled alone and every day was a new experience. Every evening I had to ask for hospitality. It's a very difficult school because one learns what the foreigner or alien experiences. When you are the one on the outside and you don't have much of anything, to knock on doors and be refused is very difficult.

'Many people mistook me for a boy because I was tall and thin and dressed in jeans and trainers. One day I knocked on the door of a Poor Clare monastery in Italy but when the sisters saw me they said "No, no, we don't accept anybody." I said "I can sleep in the corridor." "No, no," they replied, "we don't accept anybody."

'I left that place feeling very sad that they had rejected me, one of their own. As I carried on walking through the village I saw the Catholic priest. I said, "Excuse me, do you have a place where I can sleep? I'm a pilgrim and I'm walking to Jerusalem." He said "Sure, of course, come in." He made me very welcome. Just before I went to bed that night he told me that the following day he had to cele-brate Mass in the convent – the place that had turned me away, and he asked if I would like to serve at the Mass, thinking I was a boy! (In Italy, girls and women do not serve the Catholic Mass.) The sisters, however, recognised me, knew I was a woman because they had seen my pass-port, and were shocked. I had the profound sense that I needed to forgive these sisters who had turned me away from their door. Providence gives us occasions to ask for-giveness or to give forgiveness before the breaking of the bread. As the priest and I returned to the rectory, we spoke and he realised I was a girl. "If I had known," he said, "I would never have asked you to serve the Mass!" We laughed and parted on good terms.

'When I reached Rome, after five or six weeks of walk-ing, my feet were in a dreadful state. I stayed in a Carmelite monastery where Henri Catta's godmother was a nun. There are five Carmelite monasteries in Rome, yet I came to the one where this sister had been praying for Henri's conversion for years and years. He found the Lord in a sudden and marvellous way at the age of 60. This was, for me, another strong, providential sign of my monastic vocation. I stayed there for two weeks and then walked on to Assisi where I stayed for three months to pray and to seek the will of God for my future. I had many deep and far-ranging conversations with the abbess of the Poor Clare monastery in Assisi, and it was she who told me "You have a vocation for Jerusalem."

'However, staying in Assisi for so long meant that I missed being in Jerusalem for Pentecost with all the other pilgrims from France. I was not too upset about this, though; by now I sensed God had called me in a very special way and a few weeks later, in July 1984, I arrived in Jerusalem and made my way directly to the monastery of Saint Clare where I now live. I was in for a surprise because as I walked in the front door, who should come to greet me but the Poor Clare sister from Lille, Sister Marie Pierre – the one I had spoken to when I was eighteen! I was so surprised to see her, I was speechless. She said, "Well, you are finally here!" That was yet another sign that the Lord was waiting for me here. A few days later, accompanied by Sister Marie, I went to the Western Wall. There I saw Jews praying, and my eyes were opened to see the "mystery" of Israel. I cried and asked, why didn't I discover this reality in the church?

'After a time of prayer, Sister Marie Pierre opened the Bible for me to the book of Romans, and we read chapters 9–11, which describe how the wild olive tree (the Gentile believers) have been grafted into the cultivated olive tree (Christ and his people). That's when I understood that this mystery – the reality of the Jewish roots of the church – is a discrete and integral part of the church, though not a readily visible one. I realised how significant my pilgrimage had been. I had been walking up to Jerusalem in a spirit of seeking God, and when I got here he revealed this mystery to me. I later discovered that before I arrived in Jerusalem in 1984, the group from France that had called themselves "Going up to Jerusalem" had met with Reuven and Benjamin Berger (Messianic believers in Jerusalem) and held a service of repentance together. And so the moment I arrived in Jerusalem, this mystery was revealed to me: the relationship between the Christian world and the Jewish world.

'I met Reuven and Benjamin a few months later and we agreed about the unity of the church. Some people might think it strange that a Catholic should meet with Messianic Jews. For me it felt natural; but for the Messianic Jews it was not so easy because they have an inbuilt distrust of the Catholic church based on church history. So we had to start building a good relationship, and this meant commitment from both sides.

'By this time another organisation had been founded, called COEUR (heart): the Ecumenical Committee of Repentance towards the Jewish people. This was started by a Protestant brother, Henri Lefevre, and a Catholic brother, Henri Catta, the founder of Berdine, in 1989. They organised the first COEUR pilgrimage when Protestants, Catholics and members of the Orthodox churches met in Jerusalem on the evening of Yom Kippur. And on that first occasion, a hundred people gathered.

'The morning of Yom Kippur Eve, we walked in silence up the hill and through the forest from the village of Ein Karem to Yad Vashem, the Holocaust Memorial. There we met a group of rabbis and one of them chanted the Kaddish, the prayer for the dead. Then followed a lecture by the people in charge of Yad Vashem about the Holocaust. These Jerusalem pilgrimages continued for a number of years.

'Then, six years ago, a monthly prayer meeting with some Messianic Jews was started by a German Christian called Christa Behr. We agreed to meet together for a week of fasting and prayer every year. The first time was at Auschwitz. I was not there but Christa, being a German Protestant, and Reuven and Benjamin Berger, who had lost many of their family in the Holocaust, decided they should go together to Auschwitz to fast and pray. It was a symbolic act and the group went to support them. That was the beginning of these meetings between Catholics, Protestants and Messianic Jews that have continued to this day.

'This was the first time there had ever been a week of prayer and fasting with such a group of people. It was truly historic and, we believe, very significant.

'After the first meeting in Auschwitz, the next year we met in Rome, and since then this annual week of prayer and fasting has been held here in Jerusalem.

'Then something else happened that continues to this day. This group of Catholics, Messianic Jews and Protestant brothers agreed to meet regularly once a month in Jerusalem. We take it in turns to prepare a talk and then we pray together and exchange news.

'Our experiences are different yet complementary. Our Messianic brothers are very apostolic. They travel a great deal. They meet a large number of people and they give many talks. The Catholic members of the group are contemplative nuns for the most part and so are dedicated to a life of prayer, rather than external activity.

'Then in 1996 another surprising and significant thing happened. A Christian Arab joined our group: Bassem, who lives in the Old City. He added yet another dimension to the group. Our backgrounds are very different. Our points of view are very different. That's why we fast and pray when we meet, to implore God for unity despite our differences and contradictions.

'Obviously, meeting with Arab and Jewish brothers is very rich. To see that both profoundly desire peace and reconciliation whilst also acknowledging their roots and the history of their people is remarkable. Then when they beg pardon from one another, we see what is possible in God.

'What effect can such a group have on the political situation in Israel? I believe that in this group, each person is truly rooted in the history of revelation. The Bible is often forgotten or misused in everyday life and in the

political arena. The very act of meeting together and
praying together actualises the Bible for us because the
answer for the Middle East is the Old and New
Testament. Jesus is the Prince of Peace. There is a small
remnant who experience this and who wait and hope for
the promise of God and who live on a prophetic plane.

'You ask about Replacement Theology, the idea that the
church is the new Israel. As far as Replacement Theology
in the Catholic church is concerned, this is no longer
taught. The Second Vatican Council promulgated several
documents, notably *Nostra Aetate*, that outlaw and annul
the doctrine of substitution, which is the Catholic term for
this former teaching. Catholics who still hold to a theology of substitution are not in conformity with the church's
teachings and doctrines.

'However, there are many Arab Christians who hold to
Replacement Theology; it's very unusual to find an Arab
Christian who believes anything else because so much of
their thinking is understandably affected by the politics
and injustices of today.

'I believe that God has brought us together in this
group. We are united in prayer and revelation, the
prophetic word. But it's not always easy; there are times
of friction. For Bassem in particular there are painful
times. We live in faith and hope and repentance.

'What keeps us going? Hope, and faith in God's word.
He said it and he will do it.

'We tend to get very upset about timescales because
our lives are so short. But we have come to realise that
God is never in a hurry. I have come to the conclusion that
firstly we are called to live heart-to-heart with him, and
that brings unity. Intimacy with God brings humility,
patience, respect, love, the spirit of forgiveness, and unity
between believers. And of course, to live in Israel among

the Jewish people is to rediscover Jesus in all his identity and to understand that the covenant God made with Abraham and the Hebrew people is continuous and unbroken. It is through Jesus, the Messiah of Israel, that the covenant is enlarged to include all nations; Jesus is the cornerstone. He is also the stumbling block (Zech. 12), but only for a time.

'There are many people who say there will be no peace in Jerusalem until the Jewish people recognise Jesus as their Messiah.

'My message to the many Christians in the West, especially in the UK, who do not believe this, is consider what is written in the Bible. We can't understand God's plan for the Middle East unless we turn to the Scriptures and read the writings of the prophets. That the Jewish people have returned to their land is an eschatological sign to the whole world that the Coming in Glory is near (Lk. 21:24) and we are invited to enter into a time of repentance.

'Yes, I believe the fight is on for the soul of this nation of Israel; there is war on earth and also war in heaven, and what we see on earth is a reflection of the combat in heaven. I believe too that we have to pray that Israel finds her Messiah, and we should also pray for the enlightenment of Islam.'

By now it was getting dark outside and the rain continued to pour down. I was amazed at Sister Marie Yeshua's story and the candid way in which it poured out of her. Could it be that one nun, a couple of Messianic Jews, a German Christian and an Arab Christian who had been meeting to discuss and pray about their political and theological differences held the blueprint for peace in the Holy Land?

So what about the other people Sister Marie Yeshua had mentioned? Where would I find Bassem? 'He's an

optician in the Old City,' Marie told me. 'His shop is on
the corner of the Christian Quarter, just before you turn
down to the Church of the Holy Sepulchre.'

And what about Christa Behr and Benjamin Berger,
would they be prepared to tell their side of this story – a
story that has been quietly developing over the past few
years, out of sight and sound from anybody else?
Listening to Marie's story made me quite certain that I
was touching on something profoundly significant. Who
else but God would quietly bring such a diverse group of
people together and, without hurrying, allow them to
share at such a deep level and discover a desire to forgive
and be reconciled; then share what God had shown them
with other believers they could trust in order to effect a
change in political attitude and ideology, whilst at the
same time unifying the church in preparation for the second coming of Jesus?

I was now on a quest to discover if Marie's story would
be corroborated by the others. I didn't even know if they
would be prepared to talk. After all, these meetings had
taken place largely in secret. Would they agree to share
their stories with a wider audience, indeed with the
whole of the church in the West?

Benjamin Berger's story

And so it was that the next day I went to see Benjamin
Berger.

Today he is one of the pastors of the Messianic
Fellowship that meets at Christ Church in the Old City of
Jerusalem and it was there that we met, in a room at the
side of the church.

Benjamin and his brother Reuven have their own
extraordinary story to tell. They were not born in Israel;

so what brought them here? They were born into an Orthodox Jewish family in America; but today they are Messianic believers. So what happened?

Benjamin smiled, took the microphone and settled himself back into his chair; he was obviously going to enjoy telling me his story.

'I came to Israel from the US via Europe, where I came to faith after a direct encounter with the Lord. I had never heard the gospel but one day, much to my amazement, the Lord revealed himself to me supernaturally. I wasn't looking for him; but I was looking for truth. I was 26 years old, living in Denmark and working in an architect's office. After a routine day in the office, I returned home and found myself thinking about faith and realised that I'd come to a point in my life where I had no faith at all (and I came from a religious Jewish background). As I was sitting there I suddenly sensed a presence in the room that frightened me because I considered myself to be a very rational person. To make a very long story short, it was the Lord himself who was in the room and he began to speak to me and revealed himself to me as Israel's Messiah. He just spoke to me and told me that he was the Messiah of Israel and the God of Abraham, Isaac and Jacob. Of course I was utterly shocked firstly that God existed and, secondly, that God would come to me in such a personal way. Coming, as I did, from an Orthodox Jewish background, to hear that Jesus was the Messiah was very startling.

'This powerful encounter with him changed my life entirely. It put me into a crisis. I didn't know what to do. I actually battled with this issue of Jesus for about two years before I finally committed my life to him.

'One of the things God showed me at that time is that we're living in a period when God is in the process of revealing himself to the Jewish people through the Messiah, through Jesus, and I knew absolutely nothing about all this.

'Eventually it led me to come to Israel and, at the same time, I was able to lead my brother Reuven to the Lord.

'I had been to Israel twice before. The first time I came as an Orthodox Jew. The second time I came looking to see whether I wanted to live in Israel, and I decided that I didn't!

'But then when I came to Israel after meeting Yeshua, Jesus, it was entirely different and God gave me a great love for the land and for the people. And so I've been here since the beginning of 1971.

'Many of the things the Lord showed me at that time have happened. He showed me there would be many Jewish people coming to faith in Jesus in Israel, and that has happened. Thousands of Jews have come to the Lord since 1967 (and interestingly that was the year of the reunification of Jerusalem). And it was in 1967 that Jewish people world-wide started getting a revelation of Jesus, the same time as I got it, and the modern Messianic movement began.

'And so I resigned from my architectural work, and my brother and I came to live here in Israel; we believed God was calling us here. It was a time of transition and upheaval; we needed time to come to terms with what had happened to us and so, to start with, we did not work. We spent hours together studying the Scriptures and in prayer. We had to learn how to pray. Then we began to share our new-found faith with other Jewish people. We saw some remarkable things happening and some people came to faith. It was a time of getting to know who Jesus is and delving more deeply into the Scriptures, trying to see what the Scriptures say about this time in which we now live. We didn't have a teacher. We spent the time alone, just the two of us; we spent hours and hours together. Our teacher was the Holy Spirit.

'For the first five years we lived in Bethany, which is an Arab village, and God kept us there so that we would get to know the Arab people and to love them. After that we lived in Galilee for nine years, and then we moved to Jerusalem.

'When we were in Galilee, in the mid 1970s, we lived in a village in the north called Rosh Pinnah, which means 'the cornerstone'. We were sent there by God. It happened like this. One day we were praying and God gave us the name of this village very clearly. So we went to find it and at the same time we found a house to rent. In order to get to know the area and the people we worked in agriculture. It wasn't long before the Lord showed us that we were to trust him for all our needs in a very radical way, without making it known, and to begin to share our story with people in the village. They were very friendly at first and a number of people came to faith, some of them supernaturally; people had dreams and met with Jesus, then they met us and gradually a little community was born quite spontaneously. Entire families came to faith, including the children, and they were all filled with the Holy Spirit. There was a mini-revival in the town. We took the verses from the book of Acts that describe the early Jewish believers "having all things in common" literally and we began doing the same. We even had one bank account and people took what they needed.

'We lived like this for quite a while until we had some severe persecution from some religious Jews. They were not from the village but they heard about us from some other villagers who were becoming concerned that so many people were coming to faith.

'And so they attacked our house and it became a national news story.

'It was in the newspapers and on the television. As far as I know, that was the first time news about the existence of Jews who believe Jesus is the Messiah was broadcast on Israeli national television.

'We didn't get too much support; it was a pretty lonely path. However, some of the things we said at that time have come to pass. For example, in a television interview we were asked what we thought this new movement signified. We said that we anticipated there would be more and more Jewish people in this land who would come to faith in the future and there would eventually be a Messianic movement in Israel. And that has happened.

'We later went to live in Tiberias, where we were involved in starting the fellowship that exists there today. And then we came to Jerusalem, as a community. Our initial call was not to be pastors but to live in community and be a catalyst for the formation of other communities here in Jerusalem. We believed the church was to be more an expression of community than just a series of meetings. We went through some very difficult times with regard to that.

'We still live in community today. There are four of us living currently in our house, and in our congregation we encourage people to go the way of community. We have house groups and there are a number of people who want to begin to share their lives together. So I think that within the next year some little community cells will be born within the congregation.

I could hardly believe Germans could be believers

'I have been very involved in the whole issue of reconciliation because I come from a Holocaust background. My grandparents were killed in the Holocaust, and large parts of our family were killed in Auschwitz in 1942.

'So after I became a believer and I met German believers for the first time, it was very, very challenging for me because I could hardly believe Germans could be believers. How could people who came from a nation that perpetrated what it did as a so-called "Christian" nation really be Christians?

'But God began to show me something that challenged my thinking. My brother and I met some German Christians who belonged to the Evangelical Sisters of Mary of Darmstadt. This movement was founded by Mother Basilea Schlink after the Second World War. From the beginning of their work they had a revelation of God's calling to the Jewish people and went through deep repentance after the war. They were probably the first Christian group in Germany to do this and still today they have a very strong call in this direction.

'We met them here in Jerusalem and eventually my brother Reuven began working in one of their houses that offers Holocaust survivors the gift of a two-week vacation. Reuven worked there for about a year and a half and this opened up for us the whole issue of forgiveness and reconciliation with German Christians, because we did meet people there who in their youth had been involved in the Hitler Youth Movement but who had since gone through a deep repentance and come to understand, helped by Mother Basilea Schlink, the place of Israel in God's plan for the world. And not just that, we realised they had a real love for the Jewish people and a prophetic view of the salvation of the nation of Israel.

'These things happened gradually, but a door began to open for us and over the years I began getting invitations to visit Germany. At the same time I realised I didn't really want to deal with this issue because it was so painful. But over the years the Spirit of God spoke to me and in 1995, together with Christa Behr, the sister in our congregation who is German, we held a number of services at different places in Germany where there had been concentration camps.

'With Christa's help we invited German Christians who lived in each area to come and join with us. And then we discovered something else. Although it was fifty years since the end of the war, many people who lived in areas where atrocities had taken place had dark secrets in their hearts, things they had not talked about to anybody; now they wanted to be unburdened and they began confessing these things. And the challenge to me as a Jew was to extend forgiveness to them. I have to say, it was only possible through the power of God because some of the things they were confessing, things they had been involved in themselves, things they had witnessed, the times they had turned their head, shocked and saddened me.

'This was a very important time in my life and I realised the importance of forgiving these things. These people had been carrying memories and guilt for so long it was crushing them; and for them to be able to know that God forgives and that a Jew extends forgiveness to them was important to them, and for me as well, because I realised it was only the mercy and goodness of God that was making this possible.

'My parents escaped from Germany during the war. My father was a German Jew, and he fled in 1938 to Belgium. My mother was born in Austria and her family fled to Belgium, where my parents met. My father was then able to get to the US because he had family there already and was able to bring my mother over to join him.

'It was a different story, however, for my grandparents, who were still in Belgium. As things were getting worse they tried to get into Switzerland. But at that time the Swiss were handing Jews over to the Nazis, and that's what happened to my grandparents. They came to the Swiss border (we know this because my aunt who was in Switzerland received a postcard from them but she never saw them) and were deported to a place called Drancy in France. From Drancy, in November 1942, they were sent to Auschwitz, where they were killed. We never knew exactly what had happened to them until I went to Yad Vashem in the mid-1980s and they allowed me to look into the microfilm, where I found my grandparents listed with the date of their deportation. Later on I went to Auschwitz on a number of occasions and gradually pieced the story together.

'And so, over the years, the whole issue of reconciliation began developing in my mind, including the matter of the church's attitude towards the Jewish people throughout history.

'In 1997 we organised a meeting in Rome and invited representatives from different parts of the church – Protestant, Lutheran and Catholic. We didn't plan what we were going to do. We just got together for a week in a place on the outskirts of Rome to pray and fast and see what God was going to do.

'Sister Marie Yeshua was with us as well as another sister who was originally from Nazareth. When she was a child her family fled to Lebanon and she eventually founded a monastery in Syria. We had other Catholics there who hold significant positions in the Catholic church.

'We were a small group, maybe thirty. We led it, my brother and myself, along with Christa Behr, the German sister, and a Catholic priest called Peter Hocken, who was from England. The Spirit of God began to move and people started to address church history and began repenting as they realised what had actually happened; how the Jewish people were basically stripped by the church and how the church, in a sense, had lost its own identity because it had become disconnected from its Jewish origins. People from the Catholic church realised that the Jewish identity of Mary the mother of Jesus had been lost, as had that of the apostles – many people no longer related to the fact that they were Jews. These things became very clear to us at that time. At first the Protestants were able to repent, but the Catholics had a hard time repenting because of some teaching in the Catholic church that the church cannot sin: she is the Bride of Christ, and while members of the church could sin, she herself could not.

'Eventually we did have a breakthrough with the Catholics; it took longer but something happened and there was a real spirit of repentance.

'Then one day we went to the Arch of Titus in Rome, where the relief shows the candelabra being carried out of Jerusalem, and we prayed there that as the glory had departed from Jerusalem then, so through repentance a door would be opened for the glory to come back to Jerusalem.

We were summoned to the Vatican

'Then something else of significance happened: some officials in the Vatican heard about our meeting because some of the people who were with us had connections there. So it was that we were summoned to the Vatican, where we met first with the Theologian to the Pope. He was very interested in Reuven and me because he knew very little about the Messianic movement. He asked us if we would like to meet the Pope. We said that if we did meet the Pope we would want to really speak with him and not just shake his hand. And we left it at that.

'We returned to Jerusalem and a few months later received a fax from the Vatican inviting us to Rome to meet the Pope. We spent thirty minutes with him in January 1998. He wanted to know who we were and we said we were Jews who believed in Jesus; he specifically wanted to hear about this. This was before his visit to Jerusalem in 2000. We also talked about the issue of anti-Semitism in the church and how this was a tremendous obstacle for Jews in their search to find out the truth about Jesus. And he was very interested; he did a lot of listening. It was a very informal meeting; a very friendly meeting.

'So this whole process of prayer and fasting began, and we've met once a year since that time. There are usually between thirty and fifty people and we spend a week together waiting on God and listening to the Lord. It's been a very interesting experience because the whole issue of the church being the Bride of Christ, and the preparation of Christ's Bride before the second coming, has become a major issue that the Holy Spirit has been speaking to us about over the years; there is a strong prophetic dimension to these meetings.

'These people are folk who have been walking this journey with us over the years and continuity has proved to be important in making progress and building trust. We believe we've gained an understanding of what is in the heart of God for his church, and the prophetic place of Jerusalem in the end times.

'In addition to this annual meeting, we have a smaller group that meets locally every month (this has been going

on for four or five years now) and from time to time we
meet for prayer and fasting over two or three days. It con-
sists primarily, but not exclusively, of Roman Catholics
and Messianic Jews (including Sister Marie Yeshua). We
meet to worship the Lord and share what's happening in
our lives, to get to know each other and to pray. And my
relationship with Marie Yeshua is basically within that
context. She's unique in being a nun and carrying the
name Yeshua, which is the name of Jesus in Hebrew, and
carrying Israel very much in her heart and in her prayers.

'One of the things we Messianic believers have in common with the Catholics (and it must seem a strange
alliance!) is that the Catholic church has a sense of the continuity of the church; the understanding the Catholics have is
of apostolic succession beginning with Peter and continuing
up to the present time. Continuity and history are something that Jews appreciate too. Added to this is the whole
issue of the split that took place in early church history
between the church of the Gentiles and the church of the
Jews. For the Catholics this is a very big challenge because
they think in terms of continuity – an unbroken chain from
Peter to the present Pope. The presence of Messianic Jews
poses a challenge to Catholics because it demonstrates there
was an initial break that took place in the church, followed
by all the other divisions that have occurred since. But the
first break was between the Jews and the Gentiles.

'This original break is one of the major points that we
address, together with the consequences of that break,
which resulted in more and more division in the church
down through the centuries. We stress the importance of
Romans 11 and Paul's picture of the cultivated olive tree
and the branches that have been grafted in: a picture of
the unity of the church, because all the branches are
grafted into one tree.

'And so the mystery of Israel and the emergence of the Messianic movement gives you a whole new point of focus because if this olive tree is once again in existence, and branches are being grafted in, that's where we will find genuine unity in the church – the united Body of Christ.

'So this is the process that we are involved in!

Bassem Adranly and Arab Christians

'We met Bassem a number of years ago and the issue of the relationship between Jewish believers and Arab believers has always been very important for us. We quickly came to understand that what is important is that we are not threatened by each other and are open to God's way of dealing in this part of the world. This is often a very difficult issue for Arab Christians because the whole question of Israel can be very threatening, especially to Arab believers in the West Bank. So, often you find that when Jewish and Arab believers get together, they never touch on these issues because they are too hot.

'We first met Bassem six years ago and we recognised in him a readiness to be open with us and to deal with things that are usually taboo.

'He was born in the Old City into a Greek Orthodox family. Over the years we have developed a deep friendship with him and his wife (who is an American and grew up here), so that now we can talk about anything. And we can pray about anything. We have come to the place where we trust each other in the Lord; it's not thus far and no further, it's a fellowship and trust that can go all the way. That's what we were looking for, and I think they were too.

'So we are a very small group, but it's very precious because it operates on a level where we can talk about

God's prophetic purposes without anybody being threatened, even though on the Arab side they have great problems with this area. But because we trust in the Lord and in his sovereignty and goodness, and because we believe that whatever his plan is, it's not to the exclusion of anybody, we work for the inclusion of all and strive to reach that place of deep unity. We meet every other week here at Christ Church and we pray together.

'The thing God has put into our hearts the most is to understand the mystery about the Bride of Christ; this body of people from different parts of the world and Israel coming together, not in a superficial unity but in a deep unity, a deep love and sharing of life together – that's what we're believing for.

'And as for our little group, we hope that somehow we'll provide a model for the church worldwide.

Our life is a life of faith

'For Reuven and myself, our life is a life of faith. We have no newsletters, we have no publicity whatsoever; we have learned to trust God. All that we do, the weeks of prayer and fasting, happens quietly. There are no glossy brochures; there is nothing except maybe a simple letter of invitation explaining what we're doing – that's it. We keep everything on a very basic level because we believe that reflects the nature of Jesus. We need a certain simplicity. We don't believe in the Western way of thinking where things are done in a very showy way. So, yes, until now only those who are involved know about it.

'I believe that all life begins with a seed and in that seed is everything that is needed for there to be a tree; all the ingredients are in the seed. So my approach to things (and I believe this is consistent with the teachings of Jesus, because Jesus talks about the mustard seed) is that if God can demonstrate his divine pattern through a small group of people who come together and somehow express the life of the church in its fullness within a seed form, I believe he will water that seed and it will grow. I believe it has to do with an outpouring of the Holy Spirit. But I do believe there has to be a proper foundation. In many parts of the church there isn't a clear understanding of what this "whole" is; and this is the crux of the issue. It's vital that we come together to get a vision of the plan of God's purposes and then live it out to the extent that we can; to the extent that God gives us the grace to do it. I believe that if that begins to be established, the Lord will give the increase. And of course it involves the church worldwide, so that before the second coming of the Lord there will be a Bride that is ready and that will express the fullness of salvation that Jesus brought.

'There are a number of Scriptures that inspire us. Paul's letter to the church in Ephesus is very important, especially where he talks (in chapter 2) about the Gentiles who were far off but have come into the commonwealth of Israel; how the two have become one new man in Christ and the wall of hostility broken down.

'There are verses in the Old Testament too that have to do with wholeness – the wholeness of God and the wholeness of the people of God. I believe this is mentioned in the New Testament too, but the church has missed it for the most part. If we don't have a vision we don't see the pattern. It's like Moses: before he could build a tabernacle, the Lord took him up the mountain and showed him the pattern. We have to see the pattern. We have to understand how the parts fit together. We have to live it out. And that's the essence of what my life is involved with.

'So today we have increasing numbers of Jewish people knowing their Messiah. We are a new movement and, in my opinion, there are certain dangers in the Messianic movement. One of the problems Jews have when they come to faith is that they have an identity crisis. They say "Who am I? The Jews say you are no longer a Jew." They look at church history and they can't identify with it. So they try to create their own identity; and the creation of this identity is usually closely related to traditional rabbinic Judaism. This creates new tensions because the nature of Messianic belief goes much deeper than the way I dress or even the way I sing. So when searching for their own Messianic identity, rather than seeking to be united with the worldwide church, the Messianic movement has tended to form another denomination – a Messianic denomination.

'However, despite the dangers, my observation is that within the Messianic movement there is that little core that is somehow getting a vision of who we are, not only in ourselves but who we are in relation to the whole, and what our role is in the whole. It's very disorganised! I'm not a person who belongs to all kinds of organisations and I hesitate to do so because I feel we're on a journey and I don't think that we can afford to get fixed into any-thing right now; that would slow the process down. So if you ask me how we worship, for example, I would say we do things in a certain way today, but it's never fixed, it can change and we have to be ready to move with the Spirit because this is a new thing that God is doing. It's like a baby that's being formed in the womb: it has to go through a lengthy process of development until it's ready to be born. Likewise, we have to go through a similar process and if we get fixed now we'll stop that process.

'I sense that time is short. On the political level things can't continue like this indefinitely: something is going to explode. And I feel in terms of the church, too, that time is short. God is waiting for this thing to be born, something that has the potential to bring the whole together. We've missed it time and time again. I'm not saying that we have yet found it, but I am saying the Holy Spirit is moving us in that direction and the Lord will bring something to birth by his Spirit.

'I believe at some point it will become a public display of unity, but I don't believe it's going to happen in the way that we are used to in Western Christendom through big conferences or through people who are "stars". It's not that I'm excluding anybody, but I just don't think God is going to use the methods of the world to bring this forth. It's like when Jesus was born: his birth was a very hidden thing, a very obscure thing. The pomp of the world was not involved in it. And I believe that this "child" that is to be born will be born in a similar way.

'We have found that our work happens best on an individual, relational basis. When we were invited to meet the Pope, it happened because we had some contacts there and they knew about us. For example, we have contact with a Catholic community in Italy where we have very deep fellowship. Some of the brothers lived with us for eight months in our home. Some people may find this surprising until you realise we didn't get together on the basis of doctrine, we got together because we just felt God wanted us to get together. And we understood that if God wants us to grow in unity we can't start arguing about this point and that point, because that would only cause more division. We had to allow the Holy Spirit to bring us together in order to share our lives together. So when a group of leaders came recently from Italy for no other reason than to spend one week with us in fellowship, we ate together, prayed together, travelled together, shared

together and experienced a deep unity with nothing sep-
arating us. And I believe that's the key: allowing the Spirit
to move without us putting up barriers and saying we'll
go so far but no further because of church doctrine. I
believe that's the way the Body of Christ will come
together. I see it works.

Let go of your prejudices

'Of course, God's purposes are for all who belong to Jesus.
The problem is that the church has often not gone into
things in depth or has adopted certain attitudes of the
world that have become tremendous hindrances to its
perception of what God is doing. Take Britain, for example, and the prejudices that many there have towards
Israel. I think part of it has to do with the Mandate time
and what happened after the British Mandate. It was a
humiliation for the British and consequently there's a barrier. Hence Replacement Theology is quite strong in the
church in Britain and, as a result, there is a barrier preventing people from really seeing what God is doing and
what his plan and purposes are. Maybe the church in the
UK needs to repent not only over the British Mandate
time but also over her relationship with the Jewish people
throughout history. If the church would just be open and
trust God and his plan and allow him to remove certain
prejudices, everybody would benefit, because God's plan
is to bless all. And the reason we don't get blessed is
because we put up barriers preventing the Holy Spirit
from taking us further. So to the people in Europe and in
Britain I would say, be ready to take the risk of letting go
of your prejudices. Ask God to show you where you are
prejudiced and then allow the Lord to open up his wonderful plan, because whatever God has planned, it's his

heart's desire to include all – all who belong to him – so that nobody will be left out of the marriage feast, so that all might come in wearing the wedding garment. One of the tactics of the devil is to deceive people. The issue of Israel is a crucial issue; the whole world is talking about Israel. God has allowed this to happen; it's a mystery, there's a secret behind it all. And if people would only allow the Lord to show them what this is, they would see.

'Of course, we have many examples of people who were closed and prejudiced but whose eyes were suddenly opened. We talk about the blindness of the Jews and the veil that's over the eyes of the Jewish people who do not see Jesus, but we know there's a veil over the eyes of the church as well: it cannot see God's purposes for Israel. The whole mystery of unity is connected to Israel. So, if people are really desiring to see the unity of the body of Messiah and the preparation of the Bride, but they exclude Israel, I believe they will miss it.'

In pursuit

And so I left Christ Church that afternoon with a sense of having engaged in one of the most important conversations of my life. I had to take Benjamin's story seriously. It fitted in with what Sister Marie Yeshua was talking about, but it was not just a theological statement; he was describing his own true story. I was excited to be hearing about things that God was doing amongst a few people that seemed so important for the time in which we live. When Benjamin described the birth of Jesus as being without worldly pomp and ceremony, I couldn't help feeling that it was just God's style to develop a blueprint for unity in the church between Jews and Gentiles that would have profound consequences for the church worldwide through a nun from France, an Arab optician, a former Orthodox Jew and a German Christian! My time in Jerusalem was running out; I had to pursue this story and went in search of Bassem Adranly. Would he speak to me?

Bassem Adranly's story

Having spoken to Benjamin at Christ Church, I followed Marie's directions and found Bassem's shop, but there was no sign of Bassem himself. I was told he was in the north of the country for a couple of days and would be back on Sunday. I was leaving on Monday. Marie had given me his mobile number, so I called and explained and asked if we could meet.

I find conversations like this can be difficult: it's always easier if somebody else makes the introductions; it helps people feel more at ease, especially in a country where there is much fear and distrust. For all Bassem knew, I was an inquisitive journalist who could do a lot of damage. After all, the reconciliatory work he was involved in with Benjamin and Sister Marie was costly. It was pushing him to his limits, and probably beyond them.

He sounded softly spoken on the phone and he agreed to meet me at the American Colony Hotel on the Sunday afternoon. My favourite hotel in Jerusalem, it's one of the few places there where anybody can go and feel at ease (although as it's situated in East Jerusalem with its predominantly Arab population, some Jewish people feel afraid to drive in the area).

He arrived with his wife Jesura (they had been married for two years) and we settled down to talk over mint tea in the courtyard restaurant.

Bassem told me he was born in 1966 in the Old City of Jerusalem and grew up there. His parents were Greek

Orthodox and Bassem was sent to Terra Santa, the Catholic school.

His father was an optician and so, when he left school, Bassem followed in his footsteps and studied Optics at an Israeli college in Tel Aviv, followed by one year at Bar Elan University – 'a very religious university', Bassem told me.

It seems to be a characteristic of the Holy Land that you are judged by your faith: everybody is something and it isn't long before the conversation comes round to this way of thinking.

In Bassem's case, he told me, he 'came to faith in 1995 through a Messianic congregation'.

I had not heard of this happening before. The congregation concerned meets at the YMCA in West Jerusalem and is called the King of Kings congregation.

'I was hanging around the YMCA and I saw nice girls going in, so I went in. But when I saw the way they worshipped in Hebrew and prayed for Israel, I was so angry and disgusted, I left immediately. For me, as a Palestinian, it was very hard to understand how Christians could pray for Israel and for the Israeli Defence Forces; to me it seemed very Zionist. However, the next week I went back and I kept going although I hated it so much.

'I believe the Lord kept me there and he really worked on my heart. When I became a Christian, I was still going to the Greek Orthodox church and I also used to go to a very conservative Baptist church – all at the same time! So the combination of the three together posed a big dilemma for me.

'From the start, I noticed how many divisions there were in the church between the different denominations and between Jewish and Arab believers, and I had so many questions as to why this should be. The Lord gave me special grace to try to understand people, to try to have a more godly perspective about their heart and about how the Lord looked at things.

'I remained in the King of Kings congregation for two years, even though I found many things were hard to accept. I remember that I wrote two letters to the leaders of the congregation and they invited me to come and talk with them, which resulted in certain changes. Their understanding was amazing for me.

'I had been a nationalist all my life up to then. I had studied the history of this land and Zionism and I found it very hard to combine Christianity and Zionism, especially as I couldn't find a foundation for Zionism in the Old Testament. When a Palestinian hears the term 'Biblical Zionism', it provokes a reaction because for us, as a nation, it was this movement that destroyed us. It scattered us. We have refugees in Lebanon, Syria, Egypt and Jordan. Seventy-five per cent of the nation became refugees. And every family here has houses that were taken. So it's very hard for me to understand it.

'But as I started to relate more to people about their heart and about their faith, and about the Lord's heart to bring them together around him, not around anything else or any other plans, my thinking started to change.

'Eventually I left the King of Kings congregation, not because I didn't agree with them but rather because it was time to move on. I joined the Alliance Church here in the Old City and that's where I met Jesura.'

Jesura's story

Jesura was originally from the US. Her parents are missionaries with the Christian Missionary Alliance and moved to work in the Middle East when Jesura was five weeks old.

'We came to Jerusalem in 1985 and my parents began working with the Alliance Church in the Old City. Later they left to go to a new ministry, but because I had grown up in that congregation I felt I belonged there and decided to stay. It was my congregation. I went to Arab schools and much of the time I spent at school was during the *intifada*. It was difficult for my parents to keep me in the school system because there was so much focus on Palestinian nationalism. There were many strike days. Often the shops were closed. Sometimes we'd go a whole year and have half the amount of schooling we should have had in that year: by 12 noon, everybody would have to leave school and be on their way home because the transportation had to be shut down. The shops also had to be closed by that time. And whenever someone was killed, or there was a martyr, there would be a three-day shutdown when schools and shops would be closed. You never knew when this would happen, so the teachers had no warning about giving students extra homework to cover these days. As a result, the three days would be spent with nothing to do. Although those experiences influenced me a lot during my childhood, I didn't grow up with hatred towards the Jewish people because I learnt from my parents that we had to accept all. And they themselves had a heart for the Jewish people, not just for the Palestinians.

'So whilst I did not grow up with hatred, I did not grow up with a love for Jewish people. I'd lived in the West Bank and been with kids who wanted to throw rocks at the Israeli jeeps. It was after I met Bassem and we got engaged that the Lord started to work in my

heart concerning my attitude. I really attribute that to
Bassem because the Lord worked on his heart and got
him to a new place, and then used that to work in my
own life.'

New thinking

So whilst Marie Yeshua had been walking from Lille to
Jerusalem, and whilst Benjamin and his brother Reuven had
been starting their new life in Israel, Bassem was a young
boy at school. Nevertheless, here he was moving in this significant circle of Jewish believers, Catholics and German
Christians, most of whom were old enough to be his parents. Did he represent a new breed of thinking amongst
young Arab Christians at a time when tension and hatred in
the Middle East had never been fiercer? If this was the case,
Bassem Adranly was sticking his head high above the
proverbial parapet. There are many Arab Christians living
both in Israel and in the West Bank, but it's rare to find any
who take Bassem's position and dialogue with Jewish
believers, let alone study biblical prophecy and pray together. So who and what had influenced his thinking?

'When I became a Christian I started to read the New
Testament and it challenged me. I came to the passage
that says, "Love your enemy". The Lord was speaking to
my heart: "Bassem, you hate the Jewish people." "But
Lord, they do this, they do that." "Bassem, I'm not talking
about them, I'm talking about you." The next week I did-
n't go to church (I was still going to the King of Kings congregation at the YMCA). The week after that I went and I
couldn't stand it. And then I was convinced I would never
go there again. I tried to go somewhere else but either I
went on the wrong day or I went at the wrong time. It
never worked out.

'So I found myself back at the King of Kings. There was something pulling me. That week it was a good message and the Lord worked on my heart, and from that day I started to have love for the Jewish people. A few weeks later I met a group of charismatic Catholic people from America. They prayed for me to be baptised in the Holy Spirit and they prophesied to me that the Lord would use me to restore his church in the land. Since then God has helped me to understand the controversies and the lack of communication and understanding between Jewish and Arab believers.'

I was interested to know which person Bassem had interacted with and he told me it was Christa Behr, the German Christian. Her name was featuring more and more in my research.

'Christa was the one. I started to go on the fasting days about five years ago and now we meet on a regular basis. We particularly pray for the Body of Christ in Jerusalem. Then in October 2001, the Lord started to call me and Jesura to begin visiting the Arabic churches in Israel and he gave us a burden to pray for these churches. So we started to visit them and we asked the Lord how we should pray for each church. We have visited many churches now and we feel it's been in preparation for something that he is about to use us for. We feel that God is going to do something in the Arabic churches and then the Jewish churches and then he will bring them together.

'We meet with Benjamin Berger and Christa Behr every other week. We asked Benjamin to teach us what the Messianic Jews believe, because we really didn't know what they believe, and it was really a blessing. It has made it so much easier to relate more.

'We are making good progress. Galatians 2 deals with the controversy between Paul and Peter. Peter believed that the Gentiles had to become Jewish, and then they would be able to accept Christ; and he was saying that approximately fourteen years after the Ascension!

Our destiny is tied together because the Lord put us together

'I believe there is something deeper that the Lord wants us to understand and this is what makes the journey more interesting. Already we see Jewish congregations starting to mix and meet with Arabic churches. We had an interesting experience just a month ago between our church, which is Arabic, and the minister of the Alliance Church in Beer Sheva, a Messianic congregation. The meeting didn't work as we expected because the atmosphere was tense. We came to the conclusion that it was because we hadn't prepared the people properly; we never really talk about what they (the Jews) believe because in the Arabic churches we are afraid to touch on the subject of politics. The interpretation of end-time prophecies in the Old Testament regarding the future of Israel can be challenging for the Arab churches. It is important for us to understand that it is God who brought the Jewish people here and we have to pray that God will bring us together. Our destiny is tied together because the Lord put us together.'

I was surprised to hear an Arab Christian talking so candidly. I wondered how many Arab Christians would share his point of view.

'I'm sure there are a lot more than us who share this vision. I don't know, but I really feel that in every area of the country the Lord is doing the same thing and somehow he will connect people together more and more.'

Jesura added: 'People are catching the vision. Some, we sense, don't really understand it, but it's as though they are catching the idea and the desire and are wanting to hop onto the bandwagon because they know that it's going in the right direction and it's good. Also, some still have wounds in their own lives and when they try to work in the area of Arab-Jewish relations they come up against obstacles and they are hurt even more. I think we sense there are more people wanting to get involved who share the same vision, but it takes time to develop a spiritual understanding and for the wounds to be healed.'

So apart from the prayer meetings with Benjamin and Christa, what else is actually happening, I asked.

'In our church most of my preaching is prophetic. I preach about why I believe we are called the 'Alliance' Church: in Arabic it means the 'unity' church and I believe names have meanings for the Lord, they are not a coincidence. I believe the Lord will use our church to really play a role in bringing unity.

'So we are visiting Arab churches, praying and building relationships. But we are seeing that before some Arab churches can begin to interact with Jewish congregations they have a lot of work to do repairing bad relationships between themselves. We were shocked recently when we were invited to a reconciliation conference for the Arab churches in the north of the country where they have experienced a lot of conflict between themselves. There is one particular church there that split into two and then into three groups over a disagreement.'

'And again, the north is very different to the West Bank,' Jesura added. 'In the West Bank, each city is isolated. The churches in Ramallah don't have much contact with the churches in Bethlehem. The churches in Bethlehem don't have much contact with churches anywhere else. And in the rest of the West Bank there's no local church at all; it's still a barren land.'

As Sister Marie Yeshua and Benjamin Berger had shared with me about the influence of certain Scriptures on their thinking in the area of reconciliation between Jewish and Gentile believers, I asked Bassem and Jesura if they believed the unity we read about in Ephesians is possible in the Middle East today; and if it is, could it affect the political climate in the country and bring about change?

'Of course,' Bassem replied. 'It will change the whole climate. The first calling of the church is to be like salt. And even today, salt is used in the Arabic kitchen to preserve food because not all households have refrigerators. We are called to preserve the land from corruption. But if the salt gets bad it will be thrown outside and will be stepped on by people. I believe the Lord wants to prevent us reaching a stage of weakness when society and the government will step on us. Instead, the Lord wants to purify the salt so it can do its work effectively and improve conditions in the country.'

'Something we've noticed,' Jesura added, 'is that since the problems started, there's been an increase in the coming together between Jewish and Arab believers. Two or three years ago we'd hear about odd groups coming together, one or two here or there, but now it is happening more often; in fact when the current unrest started we heard about things happening every month – youth groups, congregations, conferences – and now it seems every two weeks we hear about something happening.'

'Yes,' Bassem agreed, 'what's interesting is that during the first *intifada*, which started in 1988, the body of believers was split and they wouldn't speak to each other; there were many problems between them. I heard (I wasn't a believer then) there were major disagreements between

Jewish and Arab believers. But this *intifada*, which is at
least twenty times more devastating, seems not to have
affected unity in the body at all. This means the Lord was
strengthening the believers to endure more and more
tribulation. It's interesting to see how the hand of the
Lord is working.'

It was time to meet Christa Behr: Sister Marie Yeshua
arranged our meeting. It's one of the facts of life in Israel
at the moment that people always want to know how you
heard about them. It's understandable because times are
tense. However, I think there is a positive side to this
because you are personally introduced and connected in
this deliberate way. There is an added sense of purpose
and meaning to the meeting, even a sense of urgency.

I immediately sensed this on meeting Christa Behr.

We met for the first time in January 2002, at the YMCA
in West Jerusalem where I was staying. In just a couple of
days I had met Marie Yeshua, Benjamin Berger, Bassem
Adranly, and now Christa. Why were these people willing to share their stories at this time? They had been
meeting quietly for years. Now it seemed as though they
believed something was changing. The things they had
been praying for and hoping to see were starting to happen, and it was time to look around and see if there was
anybody out there who was prepared to listen and take
them seriously. Maybe if you believe God has led you to
live in another country, or if you have had an amazing
revelation about Jesus, or if you find yourself prepared to
put aside your own political ideology and embrace 'the
enemy', you wonder why this has happened to you and
you search for people with whom you can share this mysterious experience. And it does seem mysterious. After
all, what had these people to share except their experiences? Yet their experiences had been enough to motivate

them in practical ways to change their lifestyles and follow their respective call.

Already I had seen that Marie, Benjamin and Bassem would not have met unless they had been following their individual calling; but it was in doing this that their paths did cross and then, when they dared to share their thoughts, something seemed to come alive inside them that motivated them to go on and pursue this strange thing. I couldn't help but notice these people are singleminded about exploring what they believe God has called them to do. Nothing else seems to matter to them. They are not concerned about wealth or possessions. They are all prepared to go anywhere. Their times of prayer together are of paramount importance – nothing stands in the way of their meeting.

Already in this chapter Christa Behr's name has been mentioned a number of times. So where does she see herself fitting into this story and playing her role in this process of reconciliation between nations?

Christa Behr's story

She was born in Germany in 1953. She later moved to Austria, where she lived for eighteen years and became an Austrian citizen. However, for the past twelve years, since the Gulf War, she has lived in Jerusalem. Why?

A Lutheran, she used to be a schoolteacher of Religion. Today as a German/Austrian she's involved in reconciliation and repentance for, as she put it, 'our history towards the Jewish people and our part in church history'.

'It was God who put it on my heart to pray for Israel. I felt that something had to be done to reconcile my people with the Jewish people because there is a mountain of guilt between us. Sadly, in Germany and especially in

Austria, there has been no breakthrough, even amongst Christians, to recognise and then admit the need and responsibility we have to repent as nations towards Israel.'

So if this was Christa's viewpoint, I realised she must feel a minority with other believers within her own German/Austrian Lutheran community.

As we sat drinking coffee in the YMCA, she told me how she had come to this awareness.

'I became a believer when I was 18 years old and it was just a few years later that I became interested in Israel when I listened to a cassette of a lecture from a professor in Basle. He was my tutor at the time, and he spoke about Israel's past, present and future. He also spoke about the Scripture Zechariah 2:8 that says "Whoever touches you (God's people) touches the apple of his eye." Suddenly I started to weep because as soon as I heard those words I understood that my country didn't just sin against any people, they sinned against God's people and therefore sinned against God himself. And I also understood that whether I liked it or not, I was a part of the German people. Since my youth I had wanted to be without any nationality, but at that moment I understood that although I couldn't help it, I was German, and so I decided that I wanted to do something with my life that would help to make amends for the past.

'I made careful notes of the lecture and talked about it with the group of students I was responsible for. The matter stayed in my mind and in 1977 I visited Israel for the first time. As soon as I arrived I recognised something special was happening to me. In 1981 I visited Israel a second time and I felt God was calling me to go and live there permanently, to give up my job as a teacher, leave my home and move to Jerusalem. I did not know what to do and I gave it back to the Lord in the hope that he would ask me again sometime in the future. And he did, six years later; and ten years later I moved to Israel. It's not easy for German people to face their history or to go to the concentration camps and repent there because it's very painful. As you stand in those places you begin to understand what happened to the Jewish people.'

As I listened to Christa I remembered a conversation I'd had a couple of years earlier with a Japanese friend about the day she discovered, in her twenties, the truth about what had happened to the British prisoners in Japan during the Second World War. She had described the horror and total disbelief she first experienced when she heard about the appalling treatment of POWs by the Japanese army – her own people. But this knowledge later inspired her to begin a significant work of reconciliation between British POWs and the Japanese people – a work that continues today. So I asked Christa about the day she first visited a concentration camp and fully appreciated what had happened to the Jewish people during the war at the hands of her own people.

Bergen-Belsen

'In 1993 I went with Benjamin Berger and a group of a hundred Germans to Bergen-Belsen, a concentration camp in Germany. We prayed and we felt something very significant happened: it had to do with a deeper and personal repentance. This experience stirred our spirit more than any message I had heard preached in a church on the subject of repentance. We felt the Holy Spirit was working deep within us, that there was something very significant about us going to the camp itself and praying there for forgiveness. The next year, in 1994, we decided to hold a service of repentance in all the concentration camps in West and East Germany and in Austria. But even after doing this we still felt we hadn't experienced the deep breakthrough we were looking for. So in May 1995 we went to Auschwitz again with 130 people. We spent a week there in prayer and fasting. This time was very special because we didn't have a formal programme or a preacher or speaker; instead we invited the Holy Spirit to lead our prayers each day. And although this was a landmark for all of us and many people realised the need for repentance, forgiveness and reconciliation, I cannot say we saw the breakthrough we were hoping for. We had, however, taken a big step forward.'

I suggested to Christa that many people might find it surprising that she hadn't visited a concentration camp until after she had moved from Germany to Israel. Do German people find it difficult to come to terms with their recent history?

'Yes, it is difficult, especially if you do not know that there is a God who is able to forgive. I think many people feel so helpless and ashamed about this history that unconsciously they block it out. It's very sad that it has taken fifty years for this breakthrough to happen; fifty years of silence; fifty years with only a few groups from Germany and Austria visiting the camps in Poland. The Evangelical Sisters of Mary from Darmstadt were the voice in Germany who, immediately after the war, called on the German people to repent.

'During that week in 1995, when we went to pray and fast we met each day in a Pentecostal church; we just took it day by day. From there we went into the camps and prayed. We went to the ash field and prayed for forgiveness. We wept a lot and we tried to be open to let all of this suffering come to us in a deeper way. On one of those days we read Isaiah 53

together and we saw some parallels between the suffering of
Jesus and the suffering of the Jewish people. The Jewish people went to the slaughter like sheep. They had their hair cut
off. They suffered outside the camp because the gas chambers were outside the camp. They were even singing on the
way to the gas chambers, *"Eloi, Eloi, lama sabachthani?"* ("My
God, my God, why have you forsaken me?") not knowing
that Jesus had said those same words on the cross. So I
believe the Jewish people went the way of the Messiah
although they didn't realise it. The difference was they did
not go the way of suffering out of free will.'

But if, even after this deep experience, they didn't see
the 'breakthrough' they were hoping for, I was interested
to know exactly what it was she and the others in the
group were expecting to happen.

'A national repentance does not mean that every
German and every Austrian will repent – that's unrealis-
tic. But it does mean that an openness for repentance
towards Israel would have to be demonstrated by all the
churches in Germany and Austria, whether they are
Catholics, Lutherans or Free churches. More than ninety
per cent of the German people greeted Hitler like a god,
not just five per cent. Because the majority of the population supported him, I believe, there is a national guilt
which requires a national repentance; all the churches
have to get involved in asking God's forgiveness. I think
a breakthrough will come when there is a change in the
spiritual atmosphere in these countries, beginning in the
church, when the church understands God's plan for
Israel and embraces the deep relationship, the covenant
relationship, God has with his ancient people.'

So did some churches in Germany know that Christa
and this group of Christians and Jewish believers were
there? Did she invite them to join in?

'I invited everybody who was willing to come. In the beginning more pastors from the Lutheran church came, but now, slowly, we have some open doors into the Catholic church and to the Free churches; but so far there has not been a complete breakthrough into all the churches. It needs a miracle. I know I can't do it; it can only be done by the Holy Spirit. But we believe that if there is a breakthrough in repentance and recognition of this national guilt, it would bring a national healing to Israel and healing to the church in Germany and Austria. You can compare it to a personal relationship: if I hurt someone, this person can be only reconciled with me if I ask for forgiveness. And it's important, because if you live here in Israel you meet people who are still very wounded because of the Holocaust and they have never met any German or Austrian who asked them for forgiveness. But first we have to repent towards God and ask his forgiveness.

'And why is this so important in our time? It seems that many Christians in the West do not understand the spirit that lies behind Osama bin Laden and the Islamic fundamentalist. It is the same spirit that was behind Hitler, and it's the same spirit that lay behind Haman in the book of Esther. You can compare it in biblical terms with the spirit of Amalek, because Haman was an Amalekite. And God said that the people of Israel should fight and blot out Amalek, because God is at war with Amalek from generation to generation (Ex. 17:14–16). Of course, God is not at war with people, but he is at war with this spirit. And the spirit of Amalek is the spirit that wants to annihilate the Jewish people and Christians. It is a spirit that attacked Israel from behind (Deut. 25:17–18). It was not a normal war, soldier against soldier. That was the reason why God said he wanted to blot out Amalek: because they attacked Israel from the back when they were tired coming from Egypt. It was the children, the sick and the elderly, the weak ones who were the most vulnerable who suffered first. This is precisely what Hitler did; he had no fear of God. He cheated the people as they went into the gas chambers by tricking them into believing they were going to have a shower. In Treblinka, the Nazis decorated the gas chamber with the Star of David to pretend it was a synagogue and they hung a big curtain in front of the gas chamber with a verse from Scripture written on it in large letters in Hebrew – "Open for me the gates of righteousness; I will enter and give thanks to the Lord" (Ps. 118:19). My question is, what does God think about it if a nation does those things with no fear of God and if we never repent as a nation for it?'

Christa was speaking with passion. Once again I found myself speaking to one individual who had taken seriously what she believed God was calling her to do; she had taken it upon herself to do all she could to encourage her own people to admit what her country had been involved with during the Second World War under Adolf Hitler. So, I asked her, was she telling me that this was the first time there had been any sign of repentance, and that until there is a national repentance from Germany towards Israel for the Holocaust, Israel is blocked from moving on spiritually?

'I don't want to give the impression that this is the first time repentance towards Israel by Germans has taken place in the world. Immediately after the war, and to this day, the Evangelical Sisters of Mary from Darmstadt have been a clear voice in Germany calling for repentance, and also some conferences have been called for this purpose. But it was the first time, as far as I know, that a group of German and Jewish Christians had gone to Auschwitz together.

'I also believe God is saying to us, as Mordecai said to Esther, that if you remain silent at this time, relief and deliverance for the Jews will arise from another place, but you and your father's family will perish (Esth. 4:13–14). I believe God will say to us in the church that if we do not stand with Israel at this time, "you and your house will perish".

'Mordecai also said "Do not think that just because you are in the king's house you alone of all the Jews will escape." If we as Christians are not like the salt of the earth or the light of the world, we will fall under the judgement of Jesus, just as he said. Salt that is not salty will be thrown onto the street – it is worth nothing (Mt. 5:13). If we as Christians don't stand with Israel and do what we're supposed to do, if we just say the same as the world says and the politicians say and don't stand with the Word of God and his commitment to his covenant people, we are not salt or light in the world; we make no difference.'

Christa was speaking to me calmly but with such conviction. She had obviously thought long and hard about her own position. But I wanted to know why it had taken her ten years, after that initial visit in 1981, to finally give up her job and move to Israel. What had persuaded her to believe that one woman on her own could make a difference?

'I understood that my life, as a believer, didn't belong to me and it wasn't up to me to choose where I was going to live, or whether or not I was going to marry, or what I was going to do. Initially I had a sense that God was preparing me to move from Germany to Austria. Having taken that step, the next eighteen years were spent anticipating another move. As I asked the Lord about where he wanted me to be, little by little the doors began to open and now here I am living in a house in Jerusalem.'

What makes moving to another country easier is know-ing people there. Was this the case for Christa, I won-dered?

'No, when I came the first time, I didn't know anybody. I came on a tour and the leader introduced me to some people and I followed up every contact I had. At first everything was strange and unfamiliar – the language, the culture, the tension in this city of Jerusalem – there's a strong spiritual tension in this city. But I think if you know you're supposed to be here you don't want to be anywhere else. And God confirmed it. It's not easy. But I don't want to be anywhere else because I believe he brought me here.

'Before I moved to Israel I received a word from God from John 11:49–52, where the High Priest prophesied that Jesus would die for the Jewish nation, and not only for that nation but also for the scattered children of God among the nations, to make them one. I understood that this unity was also referring to the unity between Jews and Gentiles and that this is something very deep in God's heart. This unity that Jesus died for is also related to the real peace of Jerusalem. The apostle Paul under-stood the mystery of this unity in a deep way, but I do not think the church today has really understood this.'

Christa had obviously had the same revelation that Sister Marie Yeshua, Benjamin and Reuven Berger and Bassem Adranly had received. But I wondered whether being German and a Christian had caused her problems in Jerusalem and made it difficult for her to be part of the local churches and congregations as well as of Jewish society.

'It's not so easy if you come from outside, you're a Gentile and you want to join a Messianic church and you don't speak Hebrew: I've had to persevere! There are a lot of strange people wandering around in Jerusalem, so there have been some bad experiences for the local people, and people sometimes wonder whether you're here to stay or if you'll disappear when the going gets tough. If I meet someone who has been wounded by the Germans, or they have lost a family member in the Holocaust, I have to expect that I will face some reaction. But it's not only people from Germany and Austria that are distrusted by many Jewish people, it's also Christians, because church history reminds us all that Christians have often acted in a hostile manner towards the Jews (for example the Crusaders and the Spanish Inquisition). This is a very big stumbling block which prevents Jewish people from believing that Jesus is their Messiah.

'And so I've had to learn how to win the trust of the Jewish people I meet. You can't come here and say "I've a call for unity!" You have to just be available for everything that is needed. So I personally help new immigrants when I can. I take people in who need a place to stay. I'm involved in church life and I like prayer times, because there are many issues that only God can solve; only God can intervene, heal, deliver and give a breakthrough. So I think the most important thing we can do is pray.

'Since the beginning of my time in Israel I have been involved in regular meetings with Arab Christians and Messianic Jews where we talk and pray together. In 1996 we began a monthly meeting with Catholics and Protestants because there are so many things that divide us; between traditional churches and Messianic Jews; between Arabs and Jews; Germans and Israel. There are so many areas where grace and endurance in prayer are needed in order for us to believe that God will bring us together.

'My life is so rich. I am involved in some very interesting prayer groups. The one I find most challenging is the annual week of prayer and fasting that began with the visit to Auschwitz that I've already mentioned. Now there are about fifty people in the group and when we meet we come together without a formal programme because we really want to be open to be led by the Holy Spirit and we always find God leads us to pray for some key issues. These fifty people are from Germany, France, the UK, Africa and Israel.

'I appreciate the prayer meetings with the Arab brothers and also a little prayer meeting on Mount Zion which is quite new.'

Listening to Christa confirmed my thoughts: new groups were springing into life all over Jerusalem. There is an air of excitement and anticipation that God is breathing life into his people. Connections are being made between people. A new confidence is emerging. Small beginnings maybe, but does she have the sense that God is connecting people in a very careful and special way here?

'Yes, I think there are different levels on which people connect. You can organise activities to bring people together and that is good and we enjoy fellowship together. But Benjamin, Reuven and I would like to be involved in something prophetic together, which, we believe, although very small, represents something that God will do in this city on a broader scale in the future. As far as we know, there is no other regular prayer meeting in Jerusalem where Arab brethren and Messianic Jews meet together. So even though we are a small group, we pray about some very deep and challenging issues. Potentially it could get much deeper and grow larger, but at the moment we feel we have to be a little spark or a sign that deep relationship is possible between us; we try not to be superficial or avoid certain issues. We desire to be real and honest with each other and we pray constantly that God would really help us to be an expression of the one new man in Jesus Christ that we read about in Ephesians chapter 2. We encounter a lot of resistance not only through the political situation, but also in the spiritual realm. We try to understand the root of this resistance and ask the Holy Spirit to reveal the truth to us. We try to live in a way that shows it is possible now to be an expression of this unity, and to grow in this expression. How else can the peace go out from Jerusalem if those who belong to Jesus are not deeply connected? It's very interesting that before the Holy Spirit came, the believers were all together in one room; 120 people including the women and Mary the mother of Jesus, and they were united. And as they prayed in unity, the Holy Spirit came. I think this is the key.'

It seemed as though Christa was telling me about something so new and exciting; something that had not happened since the early church had scattered from Jerusalem two thousand years ago. Could it really be that a handful of people hold the key to the future peace of Jerusalem? Had I stumbled on a small group of people who had been meeting together quietly to pray for some years, who truly believed they had a revelation from God that in order for peace to come to this troubled part of the world, believers had to live in unity and worship God together in a spirit of love and forgiveness?

Christa had told me about the group of Messianic Jews, Arab Christians and Gentiles, so what about her meetings with Sister Marie Yeshua?

'We meet once a month with a few others: in winter in my house, and in summer in Benjamin and Reuven's garden. We have a time of worship and sharing, we have a word, and then we pray together. We can see over the years how these times have got deeper and deeper. We enjoy good relationships. Marie Yeshua is someone who is known to be outspoken in her biblical understanding and relationship to Israel. We first met in 1997 and I invited her to come with us to Rome for the week of prayer and fasting. There I got to know her better because we shared a room, and since then our relationship has got deeper in the Spirit as we meet every month to pray. I think we all agree that the coming of the Lord is linked to the unity of Jews and Gentiles.

'Recently we have been thinking about the story of Joseph and Benjamin, his younger brother. Joseph had only one brother who shared the same mother and father as himself – that was Benjamin. And the Jewish people relate to Jesus as a person like Joseph, someone they have sold to the Egyptians, the Gentiles. And even though Jesus recognises his brothers, as Joseph recognised his brothers, the Jewish people do not recognise him. Joseph loved his brothers but he said to them "You will not see my face again unless your brother is with you" (Gen. 43:3).

'And I believe this is what the church has done; seeking the face of God without Benjamin, who represents the Messianic Jews who believe in Jesus. And God says "No longer! Now you have to come together before Joseph – before Jesus." And then he checks the brothers out and he gives them a reason to be jealous of Benjamin. He gives Benjamin more food and the best place at the table. If there had been no change in their hearts and they had allowed Benjamin to go to prison after he'd been caught with Joseph's silver cup, they could have shrugged their shoulders and returned to their father and made up some story that a bear had eaten him. But they didn't. This time, Judah came to Joseph and said "Benjamin is the brother our father loves the most. We cannot go back without

Benjamin; it would kill our father, so take me instead of Benjamin and let him go." And in that moment, Joseph sent all the Egyptians out of the room and revealed himself to all the brothers including Benjamin.

'I think there's a deep mystery hidden in this story, that if we stand with Israel and with the Messianic believers at this time, it will cause Jesus to be revealed to the church and to the Jewish people. There is something hidden even from the church about Jesus and the Father. After the disappearance of Joseph, their father Jacob never trusted his ten sons again; he did not receive their comfort because he knew, deep down, that something was wrong (Gen. 37:35). It was only as he heard the whole story of what had happened to Joseph, of how they had sold him and how God had made him a ruler in Egypt, that reconciliation and peace came into the relationship with the father. They had all those years of bad conscience because they knew they had lied. As this reconciliation will take place between the church and Israel, a deep unity between Jew and Gentile will take place and Jesus will reveal himself and we will really know who Jesus is. This will be the fulfilment of the Kingdom, when the church will be the Bride of Jesus – because Jesus has only one bride, not one Jewish bride and one from the nations. He will gather us as one and together we will become the Bride of Jesus.'

Our interview had come to an end. There was just one more question I wanted to ask Christa: did she sense that this process is gaining momentum today?

'I think we're moving towards it but we have to have supernatural intervention from the Holy Spirit because there are many obstacles. We have to pray that this will happen soon. If there is a breakthrough in the church in Jerusalem, it will have an effect on all churches all over the world.'

CHAPTER 4

FROM BROADWAY TO MOUNT CARMEL

'"O Lord, send your precious Jewish people home." This is what some Arab pastors pray in the north: it is difficult for them, but they do,' David Davis told me.

Arab pastors living and working in the north of Israel, praying that God would bring the Jews back to live in Israel? Could this be true, especially at a time of such heightened tension and distrust between the two communities?

If Marie Yeshua's story was about a vision in the making, the story of David and Karen Davis is about seeing a vision become a reality. And what is their vision? To see Arab and Jewish believers worshipping God together, under the same roof, completely reconciled, loving each other so that nothing comes between them, not even politics or old enmities. A dream, you might say. Well, once again I have seen it with my own eyes and the experience of being in a congregation where Arab and Jew worship God together in complete unity of mind and spirit is unique, delightful and exciting. There is an energy there that seems to take you right through the gates of heaven to the throne of God. It's as though this is the ultimate form of worship, that which God finds most acceptable and what he always planned should happen; so it stands to reason that it pleases him to see his children coming together in this way.

You may be thinking this is a crazy notion or even irrelevant. Why place so much importance on Jews and Arabs worshipping God together? Well, David and Karen Davis think it's important because of some verses in Paul's letter to the Ephesians; in fact it was these verses that persuaded them to give up the good life in New York and move to Israel.

'God himself revealed his secret plan to me. . . . God did not reveal it to previous generations, but now he has revealed it by the Holy Spirit to his holy apostles and prophets. And this is the secret plan: the Gentiles have an equal share with the Jews in all the riches inherited by God's children. Both groups have believed the Good News, and both are part of the same body and enjoy together the promise of blessings through Christ Jesus. . . . God's purpose was to show his wisdom in all its rich variety to all the rulers and authorities in the heavenly realms. They will see this when Jews and Gentiles are joined together in his church. This was his plan from all eternity, and it has now been carried out through Christ Jesus our Lord' (Eph. 3:3–6, 10–11).

I first heard about David and Karen from my friend Ray Lockhart, the former Rector of Christ Church in Jerusalem and the person who helped me initially in my quest to discover who the movers and shakers were in the land of Israel when it came to finding out what it was like to be a believer in Israel today. It was Ray who told me that David, who is American/Israeli, and Karen, an American Jew, had started a drug rehabilitation programme for Jews and Arabs in Haifa called House of

Victory. In fact, he told me the success rate of this rehab centre was second to none, and not only was it for Jews and Arabs, but they lived together under one roof, even sharing rooms. And there was another aspect to this story: David and Karen had also built, quite literally, a large, modern worship centre on the top of Mount Carmel, just above Haifa, where Jews and Arabs were meeting in large numbers to worship God together.

This couple sounded quite exceptional. To be doing all this within Israel, and particularly now, at this time of increased tension and violence, seemed remarkable. What was the secret of their rapid success?

I first met David and Karen in London in the summer of 2000 when they came onto one of my Sunday morning radio programmes on Premier. Karen is a trained singer, and they were in the UK promoting a new album. The album then was called *Behold His Glory* (it was later released under the title *Yeshua*) and contains contemporary worship songs in Hebrew and English, many of which Karen wrote herself.

The four-hour programme was in full swing and they were coming in for the final hour to tell their story. By this time I'd heard quite a lot more about David and Karen from Elizabeth Allan. Elizabeth, who has a background as a research scientist, has her own very interesting story to tell, having spent many years in the New Age movement before becoming a Christian. Subsequently she went to live in Israel for a couple of years and worked alongside David and Karen in Haifa, in particular supporting their work in prayer. How I came to meet Elizabeth is another story again. Let's just say it was a divine appointment as a result of which we immediately recognised in each other a deep interest in what God is doing in Israel today.

And so it was that when David and Karen walked into the studio, they felt strangely familiar. It struck me that David looked as though life had sculpted its own lines into his face. For many years he'd been a successful actor and director on Broadway. He had made it to the top of his profession. He had everything money could buy. With a PhD in Theatre, he was also a well-respected academic. But he told me how one night, after a successful run on Broadway, he realised his life was in fact empty, devoid of fulfilment. And, over the years, he'd become an alcoholic.

'I was acting in a play on Broadway. It was a big success, with standing ovations every night, and people wanted my autograph. But late one night, as I went home alone to my Greenwich Village apartment, the thought came to me that this fame and adulation mean nothing. The more I entertained this thought, the more meaningless my life felt. And I started to cry. I didn't realise it then, but that was the start of my search for God.

'Two years later an actor friend took me to a music studio in Times Square, New York, where a Christian fellowship had begun for actors, singers, models and dancers. As I walked into that place, before I could get to a seat, I fell on my knees and started weeping. I had a revelation of Jesus. He was all light and I was filthy. I tried to crawl away from him. As I wept I told him I was sorry. And in that instant he forgave me. I knew I was forgiven because the tremendous weight of guilt that I had been carrying was lifted off me.

'I started going to that fellowship regularly, and eventually that's where I met Karen, who is Jewish. At the same time I began to learn about what the church had done to the Jews throughout history.'

We paused to listen to a track from Karen's CD, a song that described the exodus of the Children of Israel from

Egypt and the song of victory they sang as the Red Sea parted and they crossed over on dry land. Then Karen started to tell her story.

'I was trained in music at a very early age: I studied piano, classical music and voice. As an American Jew living in New York, I really had no interest in going to live in Israel until I met Jesus. Then suddenly, for the first time in my life, I really understood what it meant to be a Jew, and the Lord put a promise in my heart that one day I would live in the land of Israel.'

I've interviewed many Jewish people who have come to believe that Jesus is in fact their Messiah, and without exception they have all experienced what I can only describe as an agony of the soul before coming through to belief. In many cases, their struggle has lasted months, sometimes years. Maybe, as Gentiles, we find it hard to understand why Jewish people have such a struggle, why they object so strongly to this man from Nazareth who claimed to be the Son of God. Invariably their prejudice is rooted in history, as the stories in this book have already described. However, I've also noticed that when Jewish people get over this obstacle, they become unshakeable in their belief and have an overwhelming urge to share what they have discovered with just about everybody. Karen explained how her thinking changed from being interested in the New Age to being a radical believer.

'Well, I had never even considered Jesus. As a musician and artist I knew there was a God, some kind of creative force behind the beauty that so moved my soul. But even in the synagogue God was never real to me and so I went on a very long search for truth and went into New Age and all sorts of other things. Jesus was the last place I considered looking. To me, as a Jew, Jesus represented Christians, and we have always considered Christians to be our enemies, people who hated us and often killed us. I had no idea that the true living God, Jesus, has an ever-lasting love for the Jewish people.'

So here we had David and Karen separately discovering their newfound faith, but they had yet to meet in New York. Before that happened, David went to Israel as a tourist and it was whilst walking around Jerusalem that he had a strange encounter with an Arab woman that was to change the course of his life. Little did he realise then that this successful actor on Broadway was about to give it all up and move away from his beloved New York to live in Israel. But, in good radio tradition, before we heard what happened next, we listened to another track from Karen's album.

'My heart longs for you, for the living God, my soul thirsts for you in a dry and thirsty land . . .'

The music ended. 'That's what we do now,' said Karen. 'We tell people about where they can find this water.'

And then we returned to David's story. 'Yes, I went on this trip to Israel before I met Karen, after I got saved, and a series of miracles happened to me there. I remember praying for an Arab woman in the Old City of Jerusalem who had breast cancer, and she was healed. I didn't realise it then but the Lord had begun to put Israel in my heart.'

He returned to New York and met Karen. The Gentile and the Jew married and it wasn't long before they visited the country together and had another encounter with the elderly Arab woman in the Old City of Jerusalem, the same woman that David had prayed for a few years earlier. It was something she said that sank deep into their hearts.

David takes up the story:

'We were called to Israel eleven years ago through the tears and travail of a broken-hearted Arab woman in the Old City of Jerusalem. As we sat listening to her, she told us about the drug problem in Israel. It was like an arrow that went into my heart and which has never come out. We went back to New York, where we were working with David Wilkerson in Times Square Church, and told him what had happened, because it was after this encounter that we believed the Lord wanted us to go to live in Israel and work with Arabs and Jews. Our role was to be reconciliatory.

'We had to know we were being called,' said David. 'We had to be sure we were hearing the voice of God. I had to leave my position as a tenured university professor as well as an actor on Broadway and TV. After much prayer and discussion with David Wilkerson, our pastor, we decided it was time I resigned from my work commitments, as we believed the Lord was calling us to Israel. A few days later I met with David and showed him my resignation letter. I'd worked in theatre and TV for over twenty years. It had become my life. It had given me my identity. But I had reached the point where I couldn't wait to give it up. It no longer held me in its spell.

'That night, as we parted, David Wilkerson called after me "Don't you ever forget to thank Jesus for your new heart." And as I walked home down Broadway, past all the theatres and bright lights, I was completely released and free; it had no hold on me any more. But you know, I still wanted the Lord to confirm his call on my life. I had to be sure we were doing the right thing.

'Soon after, one night I was in a meeting and I asked God to confirm to me one more time that he wanted Karen and me to leave New York and move to Israel. The preacher said "Open your Bible to Acts chapter 7 verse 3." So I did. And he read these words: "And God said, get out of your country and from your relatives and come to the

land that I will show you." I said "All right Lord, I sur-
render!'"

Looking at David and Karen in the studio and listening
to their story unfold was quite awesome. Their individual
stories of coming to faith, David's battle with addiction,
the knitting of their minds and hearts in wanting to give
up the good life in New York for an uncertain future in
Israel – they were risking everything. Added to that,
Karen was Jewish, yet here she was with David, a Gentile,
contemplating starting a community for drug addicts and
alcoholics, not just for Jews but for Arabs too. Did she
have compassion towards Arab people at that time?

'Until we arrived in Israel, I really hadn't had much
contact with Arab people. I'd come with this deep burden
to share the gift of life with my own people, so I was surprised when our first invitation was to this little Arab village in the north. I had prepared to sing a song called
'Behold, I'm new in Jesus', but as we approached the village I realised I felt nothing for these people. I didn't feel
angry or hostile or hateful, but I realised my heart was
completely cold and I did not have a burden for them. I
asked David to stop the car so we could pray. I knew in
my mind that God loves all people and that before him all
need to be saved, but at that point in time, minutes away
from this Arab village, I felt nothing in my heart. Then
suddenly a Scripture came into my mind from the Gospel
of Matthew, where the Lord says "If you only love those
who love you, how are you any different from the tax
collector?" That really challenged me. Jesus calls us to a
higher form of loving: he expects us to love our enemies.
So, parked on the outskirts of that Arab village in Galilee,
we prayed that the Lord would change my heart and give
me the ability to share his love with everyone. Minutes
later, as I stood before those Arab brothers and sisters,

they received me as a Jew and there was such a joy that day in being one united body in him. I knew from that day that whatever we did in Israel we needed to carry the Lord's love for all people.'

Time was running out on the programme, and in the closing minutes David and Karen described House of Victory, the home they had started for drug addicts and alcoholics in Haifa for both Jews and Arabs. In addition they mentioned how they had come to live in an old run-down villa on Mount Carmel at around the time of the Gulf War. They recalled the nights when the missiles came roaring across the sky. By this time they were the only ones living in the house: since it was in the flight path of missiles, all the other occupants had long since left out of fear for their safety. And it was then that David had another moment of inspiration. Standing on their balcony in the midst of the war, he suddenly remembered a vision the Lord had given him of Arabs and Jews worshipping together on Mount Carmel, united together as one body of people, or 'one new man' as the Bible puts it in the letter the Apostle Paul wrote to the Ephesians.

'So,' David continued, 'I asked the Lord to send me some young Arabs and Jews who wanted to work with drug addicts. Soon, three Jewish couples and an Arab couple came to me and asked me to start a Bible study. Much to my surprise, within one month there were seventy people in our sitting room and a congregation had been born. At the same time some drug addicts started to arrive; House of Victory was to be the first work for drug addicts and alcoholics run by believers in the land of Israel. An Arab would come in, hating Jews, would meet Jesus, start to love Jesus and start to love Jews – and vice versa. I could tell you story after story of reconciliation and the love of God between Arabs and Jews.'

It was time for one more piece of music. Then on with the story. Could we fit it all in before the news on the hour? I wanted to hear about how these Arab and Jewish drug addicts got on with each other. Hearing about various drug rehab centres in the UK had taught me what a difficult job this is at the best of times, but surely having these two warring groups under the one roof must have been an added tension?

'An Arab from the Old City of Jerusalem came to live with us. In fact his family lived about a hundred metres from the Arab lady who originally told us about the drug problem in Israel. I asked him if he was afraid of the pain of withdrawal. He said "No, but I'm terrified of spending a night in a house with Jews." It turned out he had been a militant Arab filled with hatred for Jews. So I prayed for him and I asked a Jewish fellow who had just come off drugs to come and join us. He'd been a major criminal in Tel Aviv, a tough guy, and I asked him to go over and pray for the Arab. At this the Arab backed up against the window and would have disappeared over the balcony but for the bars on the window. He later told me if there hadn't been bars there he would have jumped out of the window, he was so terrified. The Jewish fellow laid hands on the Arab and prayed for him. Today they are both off drugs, they've both come to the Lord, their families love the Lord, and they are both in ministry. They love Jesus and they love each other.'

With that the programme was over and I asked David and Karen if they had the time to come out for lunch. It transpired their flight was not until later that evening, so we left Premier and went round the corner to a restaurant and continued our conversation. It was clear that their vision to see reconciliation between Jews and Arabs was starting to happen. But could it last? When these former drug addicts left House of Victory, would they not drift back into their communities and former life style and attitudes? Was it realistic to expect people to maintain friendships when the country was in a state of virtual war? David and Karen were adamant that this was something beyond their power to control; what they were seeing at work in the lives of these individuals was supernatural. Addicts continued to come to House of Victory in Haifa and more and more people were coming to the Worship Centre on the top of Mount Carmel and many were becoming believers in Jesus for the first time – Jews and Arabs.

There was only one thing for it: I had to go and visit for myself and speak to those involved. Which is what happened, in July 2002.

July 2002

We were staying in Tiberias, on the western shores of the Sea of Galilee. As it was so far below sea level and we were in the height of summer, both the temperature and humidity were high. So as we steadily drove higher and higher up Mount Carmel, the atmosphere changed and became immediately fresher. It's an interesting drive along highway 77, skirting north of Nazareth and across the upper stretch of the Yizre'el Valley, otherwise known as Armageddon. To the left a road to Jenin, a Palestinian-controlled area sealed off by the Israeli army in an effort to stem the tide of suicide bombers that were constantly threatening their Israeli neighbours in Netanya and Haifa: ever-present reminders of the 'hot climate' in Israel. Living cheek by jowl, Arab and Jew, so closely related yet so far apart, separated by mistrust, hatred and fear.

Yet we were going to meet Arabs and Jews who were living together under one roof, actually sharing their lives together.

A couple of hours later and several hundred feet higher, we drove up to the Worship Centre, perched right on the ridge of Mount Carmel. Arriving at the impressive white stone circular building surrounded by a continuous balcony, we ascended the wide steps and walked into the auditorium. At once our gaze was drawn to the stage, a raised circle of white stone surrounded by twelve large boulders of natural rock. Light was cascading into the auditorium through windows in the roof.

David was sitting in one of the chairs that surrounded the stage, talking intently to a young man. When he saw us, he jumped up and welcomed us. Hearing the chatter, Karen appeared from a side room dressed in floaty silk trousers and matching shirt in a burgundy colour that perfectly complemented her dark hair. It wasn't long before the story began.

'When we started the congregation, Ray Lockhart was the director of Stella Carmel, the building next door owned by ITAC (Israel Trust of the Anglican Church). Basically ITAC gave us this land in 1997 to build a worship centre. It took us two years to build using volunteer labour. We had prayed for land on Mount Carmel because this is where Elijah confronted the false prophets and we wanted to restore the "altar of the Lord" in the same way Elijah did. He built an altar with twelve stones that represented the twelve tribes of Israel. And as we read the account of how he did this in the Bible (1 Kgs 18), the Lord showed us, step by step, what to do.

'We had an interesting team. I was a former actor and director on Broadway, New York. The architect was a Jewish believer. The engineer was an Arab Christian. And Karen, being an artist as well as a musician, became the interior decorator. We wanted it to look light. We didn't want a "churchy" look because we wanted Jews to come in here and feel comfortable: often, when they go into a traditional church building, they are reminded of the legacy of the Crusaders who came to Israel and burned Jews in their synagogues while holding crosses and singing hymns to Jesus. Part of our job is to undo the lies that Jewish people have come to believe about Jesus and let them come to realise who he really is. Jewish people don't know how to describe or what to call this place. When we adopted two young boys who'd been born in Israel, we were assigned a social worker and she once said to us "I want to come to your um, um, your house of prayer." We have come to see that people from all backgrounds feel at ease here; Orthodox Jews, Muslims and Christians all feel comfortable here.'

People may feel comfortable with the building, but what about feeling comfortable with the people inside the building; what sort of tensions arise here during your services, I wanted to know.

'We're up on the top of the mountain in a secluded residential area. As for the local Jewish people, they are just the same as Jews anywhere: on the whole they feel that Jesus has nothing to do with them and is the God of the Christians. Many are still influenced in their thinking because of what happened in the Holocaust; some of the German guards called themselves Christians (many belonged to the Catholic church). We have heard testimonies and read reports about how these guards sang *Silent Night* at the same time as sending the Jews to their death in the gas chambers.'

So are they seeing a shift in thinking? Are the Jewish people David and Karen are coming into contact with starting to ask questions about the person of Jesus?

'Yes, in the past year we have given away hundreds of copies of the *Jesus* video which Campus Crusade and others developed; it has been the best evangelistic tool ever. We've seen 120 Jews receive Yeshua in the past eighteen months. We put invitations in the mailboxes in Haifa offering this video and two thousand people replied. We believe we have a window of opportunity at the moment; it's as though something has been broken in the spiritual realm recently. Every Monday night we go out onto the public promenade in the centre of Haifa and pray over the city for its security and salvation, and people walking by stop and listen. Some have been saved.

'You see, most Jewish people are secular in their thinking and there is a hopelessness about the political situation here. In one sense that's bad, but in another sense they are open to God. It's going to get very bad, the Scriptures tell us that. But people are coming to the Lord. We read chapters in the Bible, such as Jeremiah 31 and Ezekiel 36, and we see it happening before our eyes. It's harvest time. There are more Jews and Arabs being saved in northern Israel and Mount Carmel today than at any other time since the book of Acts.'

More than in Jerusalem or in the south of the country, I asked.

'Yes, it seems there's more openness and more people coming to the Lord in northern Israel, Galilee and Mount Carmel than in Jerusalem. Jerusalem is becoming an ultra-Orthodox city; they believe it's theirs and they take a very hard line against Jesus. Many Jews became believers in the first century and there is historical and archaeological evidence that they came to the north. When the Temple was destroyed by Titus in AD 70, unlike other Jews, the Messianic Jews didn't fight against Rome because they knew Jesus had prophesied this would happen. So even then there was tension between the Messianic Jews and the religious Orthodox Jews, and as a result one of the things the Orthodox religious Jews did then was to change the name of Jesus from Yeshua to Yeshu. They removed the last vowel, thereby creating an acronym which means "may he and his memory be blotted out for ever". And today many ultra-Orthodox religious Jews call Jesus "Yeshu" and pray that his name might be blotted out for ever. I believe they have a spirit of anti-Christ in them. So that's why in Jerusalem it's a spiritual battleground. However, having said that, we know that some Orthodox Jews have become believers in Jesus. That's a big step for them to take, and it's incredible when it happens, but it is starting to happen.

'But to return to what we have been able to do in the north, we have three full-time evangelists visiting people who have expressed interest in the *Jesus* video. They are praying for people all the time and now we have cell groups all over the mountain meeting regularly. People are definitely interested.'

So, I asked, if there is a different spiritual atmosphere in Haifa, is tension between Arabs and Jews less there than elsewhere in Israel?

'Yes, and we believe that's why the Lord brought us here to start the rehabilitation work with Arabs and Jews. Also we've been praying for the security and salvation of the city of Haifa on the promenade every Monday night for over a year. We didn't have any suicide bombers here until recently; and in the two recent bombings, Arabs have been killed as well, which has caused many Arabs to ask why. One Monday night, one of our young Arab leaders was with me. His name is Joseph Haddad. I said "Joseph, you need to pray in Arabic over Haifa." And after he'd prayed in Arabic, he said to me "Hey, David, come and talk to this old Jewish man." It turned out this old man was from Iraq and spoke fluent Arabic, and he said "I'm from Iraq and I love what he prayed over the city, and he was praying in Jesus' name. It's so wonderful to hear somebody praying over Haifa in Arabic." This man was a Jew from Iraq!'

Clearly things are happening that are surprising even David and Karen. As he was talking it felt as though things were so unsettled in the country that anything could happen at any time. David continued.

'I feel that the true church of Jesus Christ is at a defining hour and God is watching us to see where we stand on Israel, Islam and the church. I believe God is going to bring Islam down (this is my understanding of Ezekiel 35); and as militant Islam crumbles, as we've seen happen recently in Afghanistan, Indonesia and Iraq, Muslims are being saved.

'At the same time, God has brought the Jewish people back to the land of Israel and now they're starting to get saved. The battle, it seems to me, is over the Koran and the Bible. The Koran says God has no son. Now that's not true. I believe any spirit that says God has no son is the spirit of anti-Christ. So we're in a battle in Israel over the truth.

'For example, the Bible clearly says that Jesus is going to return to Jerusalem: "They will look on me, the one they have pierced" (Zech. 12:10). And Jesus prophesied over Jerusalem "You will not see me again until you say, 'Blessed is he who comes in the name of the Lord'" (Mt. 23:39), and those words are being said across the land of Israel by believers today. It's so important for the church to be saying "Let God's purposes be worked out in Jerusalem and Israel" and "It's time to stand on what the Word of God says", because the political and secular world and the news media are just trying to figure out what's going on; it's not a question of information, it's a question of revelation from the Word of God. There's a pastor I meet with in Galilee who prays "Lord, send your precious Jewish people back from Russia to the Land now" – he's an Arab pastor.

'Our congregation is 50:50 Jew and Gentile, and many of the Jews are Russian-speaking immigrants. During an average week we have a prayer meeting on a Monday night on the promenade in Haifa when we pray over the city and worship the Lord publicly. On Tuesday night we have a youth meeting. On Wednesday and Thursday evenings folk meet together in their cell groups: we have fifteen cells currently meeting in homes around the mountain. Friday night sees the start of Shabbat and on Saturday we're back up here. Almost every Shabbat somebody is praying to receive the Lord: it's very exciting.'

Being a singer, Karen is responsible for leading worship in the congregation.

'Worship is such a significant part of what God has called us to do, not only to minister to him, which is our first calling, but to demonstrate our living relationship with the living God. And we find that during our worship times, many Israelis experience Jesus. They see people worshipping the Lord and they see there is something true about what they are doing, they are not making it up. When we worship the Lord there's an overflow of love and adoration out of our hearts towards God that is visible to those around us. As we worship the Lord, we read in Ephesians 2 that we "are being built together to become a dwelling in which God lives by his Spirit". And this is what happens as we come together on Shabbat, Jews and Gentiles together, Jews and Arabs together: the Spirit of

God dwells in our praises and his presence is experienced. Recently an Arab student brought her Jewish music teacher to the meeting. I met her afterwards; she had cried throughout the worship time and said "There's something real going on here." It was the first time she had experienced people worshipping Jesus and she was very moved.

'The last thing most people expect to hear about is the dynamic of Jew and Arab worshipping together. But it's a complete expression of the body of Messiah, that we are truly one in him. I believe it's one of the mysteries that have been on the heart of God since the beginning of the world that is now finally being fulfilled. Today the Jewish people and the Arabic people want peace. They walk in here and they see people loving each other and praising Jesus – he's the key.'

House of Victory

It was time to move on and meet some of the drug addicts living in House of Victory in Haifa. Before we left, David and Karen took us to see their Prayer Cave situated underneath the Worship Centre. It seemed very appropriate that such a pioneering work should quite literally be built on top of a place of prayer. We touched the bedrock. Who knows, maybe Elijah knelt here and prayed. 'Prayer happens here – just prayer,' said David. People come here from all over the world to pray. A banner on the wall read 'Pray for the peace of Jerusalem.' Once again I felt I'd touched on something truly significant. I wondered what ordinary people in Israel and the West Bank and Gaza would say if they came here and heard the stories I'd heard; or what Israeli politicians would say if they came and witnessed Jewish and Arab believers worshipping

God together, praying together and sharing their lives together. There can't be many places in the Middle East where this level of unity and harmony is enjoyed. And this was happening during a war, when there was every reason to hate.

And so we followed David and Karen and drove down the other side of the mountain into Haifa and drove up to House of Victory, or Beit Nitzachon as it's known in Hebrew. This is a place where alcoholics, drug addicts, Arabs, Jews and increasing numbers of Russian immigrants come. There's a wonderful history to this building and the building adjacent to it. As we stood in the garden overlooking the port of Haifa, under lemon and orange trees, David told me how it has been a Christian compound since the beginning of the twenti- eth century until today. The adjacent building, now used by the Christian organisation Operation Mobilisation, was built in 1898; the one used by House of Victory in the 1920s. This and other properties were originally built for a group of Christian medical missionaries from Britain, who owned them for years. When David and Karen moved there in 1990, the Gulf War was happen- ing, and the property was sold to an organisation in Switzerland that agreed to rent the house to David and Karen for their rehabilitation and reconciliatory work between Arabs and Jews.

'We feel like we're following in the footsteps of the pio- neers from Britain who went before us,' laughed David. 'A Dr Churcher lived here for fifty years and started a medical mission for Arabs and Jews. Apparently he used to go out on his donkey with his black bag and his black Bible and old Arab people in the city still remember him. Hannah Hurnard, who wrote *Hinds' Feet on High Places*, also lived here; in fact the prayer meeting where the Lord spoke to her about going out to all the Jewish villages in what was then Palestine happened in this house.'

I was intrigued to know how David and Karen had heard about this house.

'The Lord told us that the work was going to be up in the north on Mount Carmel. At the same time, the people who owned this place heard about us and asked whether we would be interested in renting the apartment at the top of the house here. And so we moved into that apartment and then discovered the history of this place. We were amazed. This property has been used to heal people in body, mind and spirit from its start in the twentieth century up to today in the twenty-first century. It's harvest time now in Israel. Hannah Hurnard didn't see much fruit, but it's happening now. So she and others who went before us sowed a lot of spiritual seed in this place. Incidentally, all the trees you see, the date palms and fig trees, olive trees, almond and grapefruit, lemon and orange trees, they were all planted by those medical missionaries.'

It was an amazing garden. While we were talking, Eric Benson, the Associate Director at the House of Victory, had joined us outside. Originally from New York, like David and Karen, he too had been a member of the church in Times Square where David Wilkerson was the pastor. Eric told me that when David was visiting the church looking for workers, they had a 'divine appointment' in June 1992.

'I had been to Israel four times before that, working on kibbutzim as a volunteer. I became fascinated by the country and began to read about the history of Israel. That led to an interest in the Bible and prophecy concerning the Jewish people and the land of Israel, and along the way I discovered the Messiah of Israel and became a born-again believer in Jesus. I don't know why, but even as a young boy I had a love for Israel. So when I became a Christian in 1982 I asked the Lord to send me to Israel, and ten years later I met David and he invited me to come here.

'I wasn't involved in drugs whilst growing up myself, but I had a sister who was, and still is, an alcoholic. I have a brother who used to be an alcoholic but he got set free. When I became a believer the Lord said to me "Israel via New York". I had just graduated from a Bible school where I had gone to prepare for going to Israel; I just knew it was going to happen one day. I didn't know how I was going to find a job in New York but I kept knocking on doors until someone said "If you want to go to New York, Teen Challenge is looking for workers." I really didn't want to work in a rehab place. However, there was nothing else on offer and I was desperate to get to New York, so finally I said to God "Well, if you want me to go to Teen Challenge, that's where I'll go." The moment I said that, an opportunity opened up for me at the New York School of Urban Ministry. What happened was that groups would come to this ministry site and I would take them onto the streets of the city where there were drug addicts and homeless people, and we would help them. I did that for three years and all the while the call to go to Israel was so strong, I wondered what I was doing in New York. I now see it was God's way of preparing me to come and work with addicts in Israel. So when David invited me here, I think I'd received the training I needed.'

Eric struck me as being a real 'can do' sort of person. I couldn't imagine him turning anybody away so I asked him what he found most challenging about working in Haifa at House of Victory.

'In the early days, we didn't have any students (that's what we call the drug addicts and alcoholics when they come here). But now we're always full and we always have a waiting list of men wanting to come in, as we have become known throughout the land of Israel. Often we have men walking up the driveway: they're drunk, they're homeless, they smell; they haven't eaten in days. We have to stop what we're doing and begin to minister to them. Even this week we took two men in off the street in this way.

'We try to have a certain procedure. We want them to know who we are and exactly how we do what we do. Also we want to know a little about their background, and why they ended up in the mess they're in. We always tell them the programme is all about Jesus, and if they want to come into our house they have to understand that we will teach them about Jesus. We have meetings every day. We believe that their deliverance and freedom will come according to the words of Jesus found in John chapter 8: "If you hold to my teaching . . . then you will know the truth, and the truth will set you free."'

That's a tough message if you're Jewish or a Muslim, I said.

'That may be true. However, we are in a ministry that is often a matter of life and death, so we don't have time to have a soft approach. That's why we say, this is who we are and this is what we do.

'We have a no-drugs policy. We say you need to have an encounter with the Holy Spirit: Jesus wants to come and meet you. So we have seen guys come in and not only have heroin withdrawal but also nicotine withdrawal. We're dealing with the power of addiction and seeing it broken through the power of the Holy Spirit. The men who are tired of their old life endure, they persevere for the full nine months of the programme. Others, however, are here for only a few days and then they leave just because they want a cigarette.

'We're learning as we go. Sometimes nine months is not enough, especially when a guy has been an addict for twenty years. They need to acquire a whole new lifestyle and so, to help them, we've introduced a second and then a third stage programme. So after nine months they move out of the main house and go downstairs, for stage two, and live in what used to be a garage that we've converted into an apartment. We then support them whilst, at the same time, they try to find a job. There's no charge to live here but we do expect them to work and we organise lists of chores and activities. This gives structure to their days, and helps encourage a responsible attitude: this is what has been lacking in their lives and it's good for the new men coming in to see what's possible with some organisation and discipline.

'When they are ready, the second stage men then move into another property (third stage) away from here and gradually become independent again.'

It was time to meet some of the men over lunch. Eric had mentioned that recently, due to the great influx of Jewish immigrants from the former Soviet Union, they had noticed a rise in Russian-speakers coming into House of Victory. One of them was Sergei, who told me his story.

Sergei's story

'I came to Israel with my wife and my son and after about a year of living in Israel I experienced my first difficulties here. Our marriage fell apart. I was an unbeliever. My wife was a Jew; I'm not Jewish. We came to Israel for economic reasons: I only really came for my son. We came from the western Ukraine where people often yelled at us or wrote "Jews get out of here" on our door. Coming to Jesus has been paradoxical for me because many Ukrainians consider themselves Christian, yet they hate the Jewish people.

'After a year in Israel I divorced my wife. I met another girl; but we broke up and I began to look for a way out of the mess I was in. It was then I started to drink heavily and use heroin. It was when I decided to stop that I realised I was addicted. I was in a hopeless situation. In order to work I needed to use drugs and to use drugs I needed to work. I quit working and started stealing and deceiving people. I was caught and put in prison for a while. In prison I came off heroin but started again once I was let out. I have often been close to death; I've been very sick. One day I took an overdose but just as I thought I was dying, I had a vision. Someone in white clothes said "How long will you abuse my patience?" Shortly afterwards I came here to House of Victory.

'When I first arrived I didn't take it seriously. I reasoned that as it was almost winter I would stay until the spring. I wasn't ready to receive the help on offer and so after a short time I left. I walked out of the gate one day, started taking drugs again and went back to my old way of life. Eventually I came to the realisation that if I didn't stop this way of life and come to the Lord I would die.

'I knew about the no-drugs policy at House of Victory. I can only say that God gave me the strength to return and this time I suffered no withdrawal effects. I learned later that people prayed for me even after I left here the first time. I returned to House of Victory a very sick man and went to hospital with an abscess on my lung. Many doctors came to see me because they hadn't seen a case like it. The doctor that diagnosed me said that in seven years of practice this was the first case he'd seen.

'After three months I was much better. I am so grateful to Eric and the people here who cared for me. I felt proud that people were seeing a change in me and were seeing something good was taking place, because drug addicts are often considered the lowest of the low. But now, for the first time in six years, I began to feel like a person again. Now I see old friends of mine on the street and they look at me and they say I'm shining with joy.

'As for my future, I want to remain in the fellowship. Of course I understand I need to work and earn money. I want to devote myself as much as possible to the congregation in any way that I can, to help needy people or distribute *Jesus* videos to people. As for my wife and son, I pray for them and I want to speak to them; I want to start the relationship again. Twelve years have passed. My son is not a child any more. I believe with God's help everything will work out for our good.'

Whilst Sergei's story was extremely moving and showed graphically the plight some Russian-speaking immigrants experience when they come to Israel, I was now to hear the stories of two more former addicts who have since left House of Victory, having successfully completed the programme. I have deliberately left their stories to the end because they are living examples of the unity that is possible between Arab and Jewish believers that David and Karen have been describing.

Danny's story

Danny is Jewish. He used to be a drug addict who thought that 'the only good Palestinians were dead Palestinians'. He lost many good friends, killed by Palestinian fighters, when he was serving in the Israeli Army. He admits that life taught him not to trust any Arabs.

When he was a young boy, difficult circumstances helped to shape Danny's character and make him the dangerous, violent man he later became. His father was violent and often beat his son: Danny can remember being woken in the morning by being punched in the face by his father. So he grew up to believe that might is right; that power comes from fighting and humiliating people.

He became a good footballer, playing for the national team. But he was also a drug addict and gradually his addiction took control of his life. He became involved in violence and gangs, he used weapons, he stabbed people. He was sent to jail.

His wife described life with Danny as like 'living with a monster'. Sometimes she didn't know where he was. She suffered from nightmares. She cried for days. She prayed for a miracle – she was a believer.

'I knew he loved me, but drugs were his first love.'

Danny stole to feed his habit and his family. But one day he made a dangerous mistake. Desperately needing more money, he stole from a friend, a 'huge criminal'. This man knew that Danny had cheated him and arranged to kill him. So Danny made arrangements to kill him first.

He told his wife he would be away for a few days. Their young son was lying on the sofa sound asleep as Danny told his wife what he planned to do. She pleaded with him not to go. 'Ask the Lord to help you,' she cried.

'Who can help me?' Danny asked.

A reply came, but not from Danny's wife. 'The Son of the Lord,' said a voice. Much to their surprise, their son, who was sound asleep, had spoken those words in response to Danny's question.

'I was so shocked,' Danny said, 'I didn't know what to do. I had to make a choice.'

Danny agreed to trust the Lord and soon afterwards arrived at House of Victory to begin the rehab programme.

But Danny hated Arabs. So when Roger arrived, an Arab from the Old City, Danny was suspicious. Eric asked Danny to look after Roger. To make it more complicated, Roger hated Jews. Things did not look promising.

After three days of tension, Danny offered to pray for Roger as he came off drugs and it was then that the trust between them started to develop. They realised they had the same problems: both were married, both had children, and both had debts.

Then when Danny saw the Holy Spirit touch Roger's life, he was surprised. 'Was it possible that Arabs could know the Lord too and be filled with the Holy Spirit?' He realised it was. He found he started to see Arabs in a new light. He no longer found himself hating them. He even started to love them. 'I can't explain how my heart changed, but it has and the Lord has done it. They are our brothers and sisters.'

Now, a few years later, Danny is a pastor and he and Roger are the best of friends.

Maron's story

Today Maron is a member of the Alliance Church in the Old City, the same church that Bassem Adranly belongs to. He's an evangelist working in Jericho in the West Bank with Campus Crusade. His life has undergone a radical change in the past few years, because until 1997 he was a drug addict and dealer in the Old City of Jerusalem.

The change started when he met somebody who used to buy a lot of drugs from him.

'I met this guy and I asked him if he would like to buy some good drugs. But he said "I'm not using drugs any more." So I asked him "What's happened to you?" because I knew him well and knew he used to be a drug addict. He really surprised me when he said "The Lord has set me free from the drugs" and he started to tell me about Jesus.

'I was amazed because he looked so different and seemed so happy and sure of himself. He told me about a place called House of Victory in Haifa. He suggested I go there, but I was quite happy with my life – I liked it the way it was. But he got me thinking. I now know it was the Lord who started to work in my life, and the Holy Spirit started to talk to me and say "Why not go to House of Victory? Why not be free from drugs?" So I started to pray and ask the Lord for help because I wanted to find this person who had spoken to me and find out more about this place in Haifa.

'Eventually I found him and told him I wanted to be free from drugs, and asked if he would help me find House of Victory. He got out his phone and called them and told them about me. I was undecided as to what I should do. I came to the conclusion that I would just go for a week or two and then leave. I was in for a surprise.

'I arrived on a Monday morning when they were in the middle of a prayer meeting. I walked in and before I had time to leave the room somebody came up to me and started to pray for me. He was crying to the Lord for me: "Release him, Lord, free him from drugs." And I thought, why is this person praying for me? He's never met me before; why is he crying for me? I felt quite overwhelmed because I saw his love, and he was Jewish.

'I found that really difficult. I had so much hatred in my heart towards Jews. I'd been brought up to hate them. I had a deep-rooted bitterness in my heart towards all Jewish people. Every Palestinian person I knew felt like I did. But slowly, slowly, I saw what the Lord was doing. I had never before met a believer from a Jewish background, a real Jew, born and brought up in Israel. It was a huge surprise to me to discover such people existed.

'Then something else happened that surprised me. One night I had a dream. In the dream I felt something so heavy on top of me that I almost stopped breathing. I was being crushed to death. I asked a fellow student to help me, but he just laughed. Then I saw David Davis enter the room. I said "David, help me." He held out his hands but he said "Maron, I cannot help you." I didn't know what to do. I was about to suffocate. Then I started to shout "Jesus, Jesus, help me, I need your help." And immediately this great weight lifted and I was filled with peace and joy. From that moment I decided to follow Jesus, and he has changed my life.

'Perhaps most surprisingly, he gave me a love for Jewish people and I now understand how much reconciliation between believers matters to God.

'I have come to see that the key to revival in our country is for Jewish and Arab believers to come together and worship the Lord. I believe we must see each other as children of God and we must love each other and bless each other. Today, if a soldier comes and asks me for my ID and he says unkind words to me, I know I must pray for this guy, that the Lord would bless him and open his eyes to see Jesus so that one day he will be my brother.

'I'll tell you something: often when I go to Jericho I meet Israeli soldiers at the checkpoint and when I speak with them and tell them I have Jesus in my life, they are surprised. I tell them I'm praying for them, and that makes them very happy. I'm sometimes asked if my work in Jericho is dangerous. I don't think so. You must love people. If you show bitterness they will not be nice to you. I have found that if I show the Israeli soldiers love and forgiveness, they always respond positively to me. I pray they will see Jesus Christ in my life.

'I am very involved in my church, the Alliance Church in the Old City. We have many cell groups in Jerusalem now: the church is growing fast. Every two weeks I meet with Benjamin and Reuven Berger and we pray together for the salvation of Jews and Arabs, that the Lord will bring us together in his church.'

Contact details for House of Victory:
Beit Nitzachon
PO Box 45384
Haifa
Israel
Email: kcarmel@netvision.net.il

If you would like to receive the House of Victory monthly prayer requests email, please contact: houseofv@netvision.net.il

CHAPTER 5

FROM ALGERIA TO JERUSALEM

In all my years of interviewing people for radio, I have heard hundreds of incredible stories, and books could have been written about many of them. However, Marcel Rebiai's story is one of the most bizarre I have ever heard. It gives new meaning to the expression 'Truth is stranger than fiction'. It is, frankly, amazing. So amazing that I dare to suggest only God could have orchestrated the events that have shaped Marcel Rebiai and kept him alive to tell the tale, because today he is a man with a story and a message that is verging on the prophetic and which is so deeply challenging to his local audience in Jerusalem that its influence is gradually spreading to other countries in the world, including Britain and the United States.

I heard about Marcel in January 2002. His name was mentioned by quite a few of the people I was interviewing for this book, as being a person whose life story mirrored his message. In other words, what he had to say about the conflict in the Middle East and the tensions between Israel, Islam and the church was also reflected in his own experience of life.

I was told he was born into a Muslim family in Algeria, so naturally, thought he was an Arab. However, he later discovered he was Jewish – and that happened a few years after he'd become a Christian!

So who is Marcel Rebiai, where is he from and what is he doing in Jerusalem?

It was to prove difficult arranging a meeting with Marcel in person because although his home is now in Jerusalem, he often travels to Switzerland and France, two countries that have played an important part in his life.

So we arranged to speak on the phone in August 2002, when I was in the UK and he was in Switzerland. We met later that year in Jerusalem when I was co-leading a tour to the Holy Land with Canon Andrew White. We had taken a party of senior church leaders from the UK, most of whom had never visited Israel before and for whom this was a fact-finding trip. We were introducing them to a number of the political and spiritual 'movers and shakers' in the Holy Land, to help them understand the complexities and challenges of living in Israel and the West Bank today. After hearing Marcel's story, I asked him if he would speak to this group. More on this later in the chapter.

On the phone, Marcel began to tell me his story, a story that started in Algeria.

'I was born in 1953 in Algeria. My father was a Muslim and he had a number of wives. He was a soldier, an officer in the Algerian army. I remember having two sisters and one brother, although we did not share the same mother. I didn't really grow up with my family because I spent many years living in children's camps somewhere in the Algerian desert.

'I sometimes try to recall my earliest memories to see if I can remember my mother or my brother and sisters; but I was only with them for a short time because when I was four or five years old I was sent away to live in a military training camp for children and never saw my family again.

'This camp was really an orphanage; we were sent there and abandoned by our families. It was a tough regime where the aim was to train us young children to be fighters, terrorists even. (These camps exist today in a number of places in the Arab world. Many Palestinian children are raised in military camps where they are taught to hate.) I was brought up to hate the Jews, the Americans and the French, even though I had no idea who these people were or what they had done to cause us to hate them.

'I remember being really unhappy, and when I was eight years old I ran away from this camp. I'd had enough. I had nothing to lose. I just had to get away from all the cruelty I was experiencing myself and witnessing happening to others every day I was there. As a child I saw tremendous cruelty. I thank God that I was strong enough in my soul and body to survive those early years in that camp. Most of the children I lived with there had nobody who cared about them. Our lives were considered worthless so we were beaten up and many were killed. We were treated like material they could work with to test their hatred and cruelty on. Quite a few of my friends were tortured. And so I decided to escape.

'I don't know how I survived but I made my way to a nearby city where I lived on the streets. My father had no idea where I was. He abandoned me when he sent me to the camp. It's hard to understand, but relationship values are very different in the Islamic culture.

'And so I became a street child. I discovered there were a lot of us in the city. We scavenged for food. We slept together in little groups for protection. My years of living in that camp had made me shrewd. I'd learnt how to survive. I lived from day to day not knowing what the future held. Two years passed. The streets became my school of life, my window on the world. I was ten years old and my view of life had been coloured by rejection, cruelty, danger and the basic fight for survival.

'Then, one day, I met a little group from Switzerland who were working in Algeria caring for street children. They walked the streets looking for us, and offered us food and clothes. Sometimes they took sick children to Switzerland for medical treatment. They were nice people and so I asked them if they would take me to Switzerland. I had no idea where Switzerland was or what it was like. But it had to be better than living on the streets, and eventually they agreed to take me.

'They managed to sort out the relevant paperwork with the Algerian authorities, which was difficult because I had no birth certificate. I had no idea when my birthday was at that time; I only found that out twenty years ago when I managed to obtain some official papers from the Algerian authorities. So until twenty years ago, my passport was printed with my "probable" birthday.

'It may sound very strange, but from the time I was first sent to live in that camp I had a deep feeling that God was with me. I can't explain why, I just know that's what I felt. I was aware of him. When I was afraid, I knew he was there and would look after me. I believe now he helped to keep me alive during those difficult and dangerous days. Many times my life was in danger. I was often hurt or sick, often unhappy and lonely; but through it all, in my worst moments, God was there.

'And so the day arrived when I was taken out of Algeria and arrived in Switzerland. I went from the desert to the mountains: it was a shock.

'In Switzerland my life changed completely. I was immediately surrounded by a lot of affection and people who really, genuinely cared for me, and this made it easy for me to settle there. They educated me too. Up to that time I had never been taught an alphabet or how   to read. It was exciting. And it was here that God started to prepare the way my life was to go through the family who were caring for me and who later officially adopted me.

'They were humanists, kind people with big hearts. Some years later my mother told me why they decided to keep me as a foster child, because when I first arrived in Switzerland they had only agreed to house me temporarily, as her husband had cancer and was very sick. This had serious financial implications for them because they ran a small business and were dependent on it for their livelihood. Even though they weren't Christians at that time, she prayed to God and said that if he healed her husband, she would keep me and look after me until I was grown up. One month later her husband was healed and he went on to live for another forty years.

'So I went to school and learnt to read and write. I was taught in German and later had to study French, so I learnt those languages very quickly. I loved to learn and thrived in this new environment. But as I approached my teenage years, I entered a difficult time. I had become very Swiss and as a result I had forgotten all my Arabic. I started to wonder who I really was and where I had come from. I didn't look Swiss, and although I spoke their language, I didn't feel I belonged there. So I started to search for an identity and I got really mixed up.

'I started to mix with the wrong company and it wasn't long before I started taking drugs. For two or three years I dealt in drugs and took heroin. Deep down I was seeking; I was experimenting. I was looking for something but I had no idea what "it" looked like. I even went back to

Algeria for six months. But even there I couldn't find what I was looking for.

'Many of my friends died through drug abuse. I was sent to prison several times. But my search continued and, strangely enough, I started to read the Bible. I found myself drawn to read it and I became fascinated by the person of Jesus. He really touched my heart. But there was so much I found difficult to understand. I suppose I was taking a philosophical approach: Jesus was an interesting person, he was unique, I appreciated his stories and his attitude, but at that point, he made no difference to my life or situation. I didn't realise it then, but what I needed was a spiritual breakthrough.

'A short while later, I found myself in prison in Switzerland awaiting trial in connection with a drugs charge, when it happened. I remember that day so clearly even now, almost thirty years later. I was lying on my bed in my cell doing absolutely nothing. I wasn't praying; the only desire I had was to smoke a cigarette. Suddenly I knew that I was not alone in my cell, but as I looked around I couldn't see anybody. It was only a small cell with nowhere for anybody to hide, but I knew there was somebody else there. What was going on? I had never experienced anything like this before. The next moment I found myself on my knees and crying the same words that Paul cried: "What do you want me to do?" I don't know how long this went on for, but it was so clear. He told me "I am the one you are looking for. I am the truth. I have always been with you. There is nowhere else to go." And that was the start of my new life. It happened just like that.

'I didn't tell anybody. Who was there to tell? Only the prison guards, and I felt they wouldn't believe me. They might think I had taken too many drugs. A few minutes later the warders came and unlocked my cell door. I was led out and driven to court and the trial started. I was expecting a long prison sentence. But the judge released me after the trial. What was happening to me? I felt strangely surprised at the outcome because they had enough evidence to keep me in prison. I'd been unexpectedly freed, however, so what was I to do now? Where should I go? Normally I would have gone straight back to my friends and my usual way of life.

'But instead, I lived quietly for two weeks thinking about all that had happened to me. I decided to contact some Christians I knew who lived together in a little Christian community. I told them what had happened to me.

'I'd known about these people for some time because folk from this community regularly came onto the streets to help addicts. I'd often spoken to them then and they remembered me.

'When I told them what had happened to me in my prison cell, they could hardly believe my story. They thought I was joking, yet they could see I had changed. I told them "Listen, I need help." Realising I was being utterly genuine, they invited me to go and live with them and be part of their community.

'After three months I had changed so much that I decided to go to the police station and admit to other crimes I'd committed in the past for which I'd never been caught. I walked into the police station and I told them "Now I have to tell you all the things I've done that you don't know about."

'I knew there was no other way to go. The Lord had told me "only the truth will make you free. And if you are willing to accept the consequences, I will make a way for you."

'I expected to get a few years in prison for all I'd done. I'd given the matter considerable thought and was prepared to suffer the consequences. In fact, I'd reached the point where I wanted to confess all the crime I'd been involved in. It was tormenting me and I wanted to be free from it. The police officer I spoke to was surprised to see me. He was even more surprised to hear I had changed and wanted to admit my past crimes. He took me into a small room, we sat down at a table and he took down my statement and arranged for me to speak with the judge who would decide my case.

'Eventually the day came to talk with the judge. There were other people in the room and I started to explain my story and why I was admitting to past crimes. As soon as I started to speak, the judge said "Listen, let us talk alone." And he sent everybody out of the room. I told him my story and when I'd finished he said to me "You did what you had to do, and now I'm going to do what I have to do." And he cancelled all the charges against me. I got up and walked out of that room a free man, thrilled at the outcome.

'I knew that God had given me my life back. I now wanted to serve him. Nothing else. I had no doubt about that. But I didn't know how or where to begin. So I embarked on what was to be a long time of searching and learning how to be a disciple of Jesus. I spent three years with the Jesus Brotherhood, a Protestant community in Germany. That was a very good time of discipleship and it helped me to gain a broad understanding about the Body of Christ, because there I lived with people from different backgrounds – Protestant, Catholic and Orthodox. Then I went back to Switzerland and studied medicine for three years, and then taught for a while before becoming a youth counsellor. All my past experience started to make sense and through the grace of God I saw a lot of young people come out of their old way of life, which often involved drug-taking, and find the Lord just as I had done.

'Then something else happened that was to change my life for ever. I fell in love and decided to get married. By now it was 1983. Little did I realise it, but I'd also reached another significant point in my life – I was about to be confronted with the truth about my family background in Algeria. I was thirty years old.

'I have to admit that although I'd had a good education in Switzerland, I had no understanding about Israel. I knew about the Middle East conflict, but I looked at it from a humanistic perspective. I even wrote articles about the possibility of Jews and Arabs living together.

'It happened like this. In order to get married in Switzerland, I had to produce my birth certificate. So I wrote a letter to the relevant authority in Algeria and requested that they send me the papers I required. I had no idea if such documents existed. Eventually, however, I received a package enclosing some documents. The information they disclosed shocked me because I discovered something about my past that I had often wondered about: my mother must have been Jewish. I could hardly believe it. After all those years, just as I was about to marry a beautiful Swiss girl, my life was turned upside down again. What was God saying to me now?

'So now, once again, I had to deal with the whole issue of my identity. To be honest, I couldn't face it because I felt there was too much emotion and religion connected with it. I was so shocked. I'd never really felt like an Arab, even though I knew my father was an Arab and a Muslim, because I'd grown up in Switzerland and had become a Westerner in my thinking. But when I was confronted with the realisation about my Jewish roots through my mother, I realised it looked as though God now wanted me to address this whole issue. So I did, in my own way. I ended up saying to the Lord "I will serve you as a missionary among Muslims. There are over a billion Muslim people in the world who need the gospel; but please spare me from this whole Jewish identity thing."

'And so we married and settled down, and I continued with my work amongst young people in Switzerland.

'However, in 1987 the Lord spoke very clearly to me again, at a time when my work amongst the youth was really prospering. The Lord said "I want you to leave what you're doing." And he spoke to me about Israel. But to be honest, I didn't want to hear about Israel. So I said "OK, Lord, I am willing to serve you and do whatever you want, but let me start with Egypt."

'So we went to Egypt. When I say "we", I mean that by this time we had six other Christians who worked with us: three men and three young women who were prepared to come with us to serve the Lord wherever he sent us. By this time we had formalized our work and were a recognized Christian ministry based in Switzerland and I had a lot of friends, people who were willing to stand behind us and support us, who believed in the calling the Lord had given us to reach Muslims with the gospel.

'We stayed about eighteen months in Egypt. At first we spent some time studying Arabic and then we lived as a small Christian community in the middle of a Muslim Brotherhood area. We had radical Muslims and fundamentalists living around us. We wanted to serve the Lord radically and during that time we saw Muslim extremists expressing an interest in reading the Bible. We were threatened many times, but the Lord always protected us.

'One day, however, things turned ugly when some of the elders from local villages started to run a hate campaign against us. It was clear they wanted to drive us away. Three of our group were arrested and put in jail in Cairo. They accused us of trying to persuade their youth away from the Islamic faith. They made out we were an organisation funded by Americans and Jews; it was a big story in the newspapers. But thank God, after five weeks our workers were released and we were able to leave the country safely. Back in the peace and safety of Switzerland we realised that the Lord was saying "Now, that's enough."

'Once again God started to talk to us about going to work in Israel. And once again I felt I wasn't ready to do that, so we went to Marseille! I considered Marseille was a good place to go because it was a city housing approximately 250,000 Muslims and 100,000 Jews from North Africa. Almost half the population of the city consisted of North African Muslims or Jews.

'We were soon able to develop a thriving ministry among Muslim children in different areas of the city, and to this day we have a significant part of our community (Community of Reconciliation) living there and working among Muslims and Jews.

Now it's Jerusalem

'In 1994, the Lord spoke to me very clearly again and said "Now it's time to go to Jerusalem." But to be honest, I was afraid to go to Jerusalem because I knew that if I went there, I would have to deal with my identity. And so it was that the Lord waited for me to be willing, and finally we went to Jerusalem. Some of the community from Marseille came with us, and to begin with we called ourselves Project Ishmael. That was until the Lord said

"Now you call it 'The Community of Reconciliation'" and he showed us that our calling was not just to the descendants of Ishmael (Muslims) but also to the Jewish people.

'I wasn't able to do that at first. However, in Jerusalem today we have managed to achieve this. We are deeply involved with the lives of many Jews and Arabs, both inside and outside Israel. This happens on an everyday basis as we try to express God's message of hope and reconciliation in word and deed through friendship, social and moral help, support and comfort.

'We have experienced massive opposition and violent assaults from both Islamic fundamentalists and Jewish Orthodox groups. But this has not stopped us. We also experience lives being changed and reconciliation and hope becoming a reality for our Jewish and Arab friends. This encourages us to fully invest our lives, because we believe according to Isaiah 19:24–25 that the day will come when God will make the two peoples a blessing for the whole world. We are working towards the fulfilment of this promise.

Three pillars

'Our life and ministry are based on three pillars:

1. Prayer for the Jewish people, for Israel and the Arab nations, because we believe that God will restore Israel and that he also has thoughts of salvation and a special calling for the Arab people.
2. Community living, because we want to be an example of God's Kingdom through the way we relate to one another, by accepting, respecting, loving and serving each other. How can we truly love Jews and Arabs if we do not love our closest family, relatives, friends and co-workers? Jesus tells us in John 13:34–35

"A new commandment I give you: Love one another. As I have loved you, so you must love one another. By this all men will know that you are my disciples, if you love one another." It's our desire that our Jewish and Arab friends will taste and see through our personal lives, our families, our integrity and love to one another, the reality of God's Kingdom and his Messiah whom we proclaim.

3. Friendship with the Jewish and the Arab people. We want to share our lives and the good news of the Jewish Messiah, Jesus, with them. We do not want to transform Jews into Christians, because believing in Jesus does not alter a person's Jewish identity. Jesus was a Jew and the first church was purely Jewish. So again today we know of many Jews who believe in Jesus as the Messiah of Israel and the Saviour of the whole world; at the same time, their identity and self-understanding remain totally Jewish.

'Being myself part of the Messianic body in Israel, it's my big desire, together with other leaders, to work towards unity, reconciliation and declared common targets for the Messianic body. Of great importance for me, of course, is also our unity with the Arab spiritual leadership.

'Efforts in this direction are being made in Jerusalem as well as on a national level, and many encouraging experiences have already helped us on our path together.

The Jews say we're not Jews and the Christians say we're not Christians

'There are also a number of challenges for us because the leadership experience many frustrations here and it's always tempting to give up. It takes people who are determined to persevere despite the difficulties. And I think it's difficult because not only is the Messianic community young and weak, but also there is an unbelievable spiritual battle going on against this tiny body. There are many distractions and demands made upon us and it's very difficult to find enough time and strength to grow.

'Added to that is the question of spiritual identity: where do we really belong? The Jews say we're not Jews any more, and the Christians say we're not Christian. We are still dealing with this issue and trying to understand the significance of the Messianic body within the people of Israel; and to see how we can be a prophetic voice today to the nation. It's a major challenge.

I believe peace can come to Israel . . .

'For me, especially with my background, the reconciliatory aspect of the work is very important because many Messianic believers are content to stay within the confines of their own Messianic fellowships and not have any contact with Arab Christians. Thank God I'm not the only Messianic leader who is deeply committed to this challenge. It's a huge challenge, because I believe:

1. Peace can only come to Israel through the Messiah. The only way to bring Jews and Arabs together in a real relationship that can stand the heat of the political climate in the Middle East is through a common belief in the Messiah. This is the only possible scenario, because both have to start seeing each other through new eyes; they have to realise there is something more than the ethnic, political issue. We are not talking here about the land, because my understanding of the Bible is that there's no doubt that the

calling of Israel is connected to the land. So, to me, there's no argument for a Palestinian State because this is not a biblical option; it's just not. However, at the same time we believe in a God who does not exclude anybody. It's his favour to include all, to give life; but it's always on his conditions, not on the conditions of the people.

2. Arabic nationalism has nothing to do with God because Arabic nationalism is always rooted in Islam. Those who are nationalistic and Arabs are such an easy target for Islam. I speak not my own ideas but according to the Word of God, which makes this clear; there is no place for Arab nationalism in Israel.

Before God there is no difference between Jews and Arabs

'Today, in this current political climate, this is a tough message to speak as well as to accept, but everywhere I go I try to explain that before God there is no difference between Jews and Arabs; the blood of the Messiah is the same for Jews and Arabs and God has nothing more precious to give than that. So there is no argument about God's love. But there is something special about his calling to different ministries, and here we have to accept God's calling.

'I think it's very important to show Arabs that God loves them in just the same way that he loves the Jewish people – there's no second and first class. Coming from my background, I understand that a deep-rooted feeling of inferiority drives Arabs. They are driven by the feeling that God threw out Ishmael; that he was expelled. But that's not true. If you read the story of Ishmael, it says that

God was with Ishmael. In his mercy, he never gave up on Ishmael. How could he? He's the God of life. When we are able to explain this and show them what God is doing in Israel, restoring Israel, that this is about salvation – salvation for the whole world – that it's not just about the Jewish people, that Arabs are part of it, they are even a tool in it, but that at the end it's about him and the salvation of the nations, their eyes are opened and they see things differently, and reconciliation becomes the desire of their hearts.

'The current *intifada* has challenged our work because before it started there were many good relationships between Jewish and Arab believers. We had many meetings and times of prayer together. Since the *intifada* a lot of this work has ceased, because on the Arab side there is a lot of fear, especially among those who live in the territories, who are not always able to travel freely.

'However, where we do see a breakthrough, despite the *intifada,* is in the area of evangelism to Muslims. Muslims, and especially their children, are much more open to the gospel than they were before. They are desperate, as are the Jewish people. They have lost all sense of hope and are crying out for God to help them. They are realising that, politically, everything has failed. I think God is using this time of trouble to break down every trust in human ability. So this is a good thing, but there is also a lot of suffering.'

What is going to happen, I asked.

'That's a good question. Actually, nobody can really say precisely what will happen. But what we can say with certainty is that God is going to use the situation in Israel to make himself known to both the Arabs and Jews who share this land. I believe the Bible warns us that things will get even worse. God has to break the belief of our

politicians in their own ability, or the ability of the army
or other friendly nations, and it is not broken yet. It may
be that God will allow even more suffering to the degree
that the nation will start to call on the name of God, to call
for help. We may yet have to face a major war. I really
believe it will become much worse because Islam will
never accept the presence of the state of Israel. God has
yet to break down and humiliate the proud spirit of
Islam. I believe the Arab nations have to wake up and
realise that it's not true that Islam is the victorious religion
of God. I believe the fall of Islam could happen like the
fall of the Iron Curtain. I do not speak here about the
whole Islamic world; I speak about the Islamic nations
surrounding Israel. I believe they have a special destiny,
different from that of the other Islamic nations, because in
Isaiah 19 God speaks very clearly about a highway, and
how there will come a day when God will link Israel with
Egypt and Assyria. He says "In that day there will be a
highway from Egypt to Assyria. . . . In that day Israel will
be the third, along with Egypt and Assyria, a blessing on
the earth. The Lord Almighty will bless them, saying,
'Blessed be Egypt my people, Assyria my handiwork, and
Israel my inheritance.'"

'I think that's why the enemy is fighting with all his
strength to stop this promise coming through. But God
has ordered this to happen.'

And that was the end of our telephone conversation. I
wondered what people would think about Marcel's
analysis of the Middle East crisis. Yet, I wondered, could
it be that his own experience of life, along with revelation
from the Holy Spirit, had given him an insight into what
God was doing and is about to do in the Middle East?

As I mentioned earlier in this chapter, I was planning to
take a group of senior church leaders to Israel a few

months later, in October. So I asked Marcel if he would be free to talk to them. I told him I would like them to hear what he had to say and see how they reacted to his story and his biblical analysis of the current situation. The majority of these church leaders hadn't been to Israel before and were genuinely seeking to take the spiritual pulse of the country. They wanted to understand this conflict for themselves and understand it in the light of the Bible.

Marcel graciously said he would speak to them if he possibly could, but at that point in time his diary was completely full and, in addition, he would be on holiday with his family around that time, time he usually guarded and let nobody interrupt.

I considered what Marcel had said and compared his experience with the other stories in this book: was a pattern emerging? Each story seemed to complement the others. Through personal trial and challenge, God seemed to be drawing a number of people to Israel to reflect his heart for this little nation and the two people groups who shared the land.

As October drew closer I started to organise the itinerary for the church leaders' visit to Israel. I called Marcel's office in Jerusalem to find out if he would be free to come and talk to our group. 'Unlikely,' came the reply. 'He's on holiday with his family during that time. But I'll ask Marcel and see what he says.'

We arrived in Jerusalem and I received a call from Marcel's office. Marcel was in Jerusalem for a couple of days and would then be going up to the Galilee region for a holiday with his family. It so happened that they would be staying just up the road from our hotel and Marcel agreed to break all his rules and bring his wife and family to have dinner with our group of church leaders and share with them his understanding of Islam, Israel and the church today. We met briefly in Jerusalem and talked further. I then saw how life had etched its lines into Marcel's face. Behind those smiling eyes and gentle exterior lay years of memories. But he struck me as a man entirely at peace with himself, the struggle to assume his rightful identity now laid to rest, and perhaps the greater struggle of sharing his message with whoever will listen challenges him now.

And so Marcel came to meet our church leaders in Galilee that night and in his quiet, gentle manner started to draw us into his understanding of what God is doing in the Middle East today. Why have I included an outline of what he said that night in this book? Well, you won't hear many people preaching this message. If he is wrong, only time will tell. However, if he is right, perhaps as Christians we may have some hard thinking to do about our position on Israel and Islam in the world today and God's purposes for both. So be prepared to have your theology and your politics challenged.

In any case, his story fits with the sentiments of other stories in this book, and is the perfect introduction for the final chapter of this book, written by R.T. Kendall, about his meeting with Yasser Arafat in 2002, a strategic meeting that he believed God arranged for him.

Israel and Islam – why do we need to hear teaching about this?

We were staying in Kibbutz Kanar, a beautiful hotel on the north-eastern shores of the Sea of Galilee. We were nearing the end of our tour, and by now our church leaders had heard nearly every argument there was to be heard on the pros and cons for peace in Israel and the

West Bank. Now they were to hear Marcel Rebiai tell his story and explain his understanding of Israel, Islam and the church. He began by suggesting we need an understanding about the spiritual reality of Islam if we are to properly understand the conflict today.

'It's very important to be aware that this is not a conflict between two ethnic groups, Israel and the Palestinians, as the media try to tell everybody. It's not even a political conflict. It's a religious conflict.'

Marcel speaks a number of languages fluently and was concerned that because English is not a language he often uses, his audience might not understand him. So he spoke slowly and chose his words carefully.

'That's why we need to try to understand what is behind this struggle the Arab nations are having against Israel. We also have to ask why the presence of the state of Israel today is such an offence, especially to the Islamic nations.

'We all know that today almost every child knows where Jerusalem is. Even if they don't know where London or Paris is, they know where Jerusalem is because it's in the news every day. And why is that? It was not the case fifty-five years ago, but today all the attention and the eyes of the world are focused on this place. Why? I believe it is because God has opened the last chapter in history and one of the main strongholds opposing God is Islam.

'Many Christians today call Islam a religion of peace. Perhaps this is because after 11 September nobody wants to get into conflict with Islam. But what is behind Islam and what is the strategy of Islam towards Israel and the church?

'Many people think Islam started in the sixth century, but I believe it started much earlier than that. I believe it started with Edom.

Who is Edom?

'In Jewish teaching Edom is the enemy of the Jewish people. Edom appears in the Word of God in connection with
Esau. Esau, the brother of Jacob, was the first-born son.
However, he believed too much in his own ability, so did
not appreciate the responsibilities associated with being
the elder son. Edom or Esau is mentioned in Hebrews 12,
where we read that God rejected him because he sold his
inheritance rights for a single meal. In other words,
because he had no respect for the Holy One, God rejected
him.

'We know that Jacob was not without his faults. His
method of obtaining the rights of the first-born was not
really kosher! But he did respect God. The Bible tells us
that when Esau realised that Jacob had cheated him out of
his rights, he hated Jacob and looked for an opportunity
to kill him. As Esau's hatred against Jacob grew, we read
that Ishmael came into the picture. It's important to see
that until this point there had been no conflict between
Ishmael and his brother Isaac. The Bible describes how
they even came together to bury their father Isaac. But
then Esau took one of Ishmael's daughters as his wife in
order to offend his mother and his father (that was in
addition to the many other foreign girls he had married).
And then two things came together, the hatred and the
power of Esau and the feeling of rejection by Ishmael.
Ishmael felt rejected by his father Abraham and by God,
even though God had promised to bless Ishmael when he
said to Abraham "Because he's your descendant, I will
bless him and make him a great nation . . . but I will give
Isaac the inheritance."

'And what is this inheritance? It is the inheritance God
gave to Abraham and his descendants through Isaac

when he said "I will bless you and make you a blessing among the nations." In other words, I will make you a place of revelation to the nations, a place where God will reveal himself to this world. God wanted to reveal himself and bring the nations to himself, but he needed a place where he could reveal himself to the nations. He chose Israel. Why?

Why did God choose Israel?

'We need to look at the person of Abraham, and then we understand why God wanted to work and to commit himself to this man and his descendants. He's an unbelievable man. I believe Abraham was the reason why God committed himself to Israel.

'When God promised that he would "be a blessing to the nations", it was not only to be a spiritual reality; the blessings of God are always concrete. God told Abraham "I will lead you to a land which I will give you."

'The land God promised Abraham was inhabited at the time, but God said "I will cast out this nation because they are evil," not because you are good, but because they are evil. "This is my place," said the Lord, "and because it's my place I will give it to you so that you may get to know me. I will deal with you in this place, in this land."

'And this is one of the main problems today: not only does Israel have a spiritual inheritance, but this spiritual inheritance is connected to a concrete land.'

Marcel went into great detail explaining the ramifications of Israel's inheritance of the land and the spiritual implications of this.

'Edom's struggle against Jacob was always connected to the inheritance,' he went on. 'Edom became the driving force and spirit that throughout history has united nations with the intention of taking away this inheritance from Israel.' He quoted from Psalm 83:5, which talks about 'the tents of Edom'. 'And then we see listed all the different tribes living in the Middle East, all led by Edom, one driving force. What is their goal? Edom, who says "Let us take possession of the pasture-lands of God" (Ps. 83:12). It's interesting to see that they understood that this land is God's; this inheritance is God's.'

Marcel then quoted another verse: Ezekiel 36:4–5. 'This is what the Sovereign Lord says to the mountains and hills, to the ravines and valleys, to the desolate ruins and the deserted towns that have been plundered and ridiculed by the rest of the nations around you – this is what the Sovereign Lord says: In my burning zeal I have spoken against the rest of the nations, and against Edom, for with glee and with malice in their hearts they made my land their own possession so that they might plunder its pasture-land.'

'Brothers and sisters,' said Marcel, 'that's not politics, that's the Word of God, and we have to understand that the world will always be in conflict with God about this place (Israel). It's not because Israel has taken this land, but because this land is God's and God said "I decided to reveal myself from this place, through this nation, and all the nations will see it."

'So what we are seeing today is a struggle between the Spirit of God and the Spirit of Edom.'

Marcel then gave us some Scriptures to support his case to show us how Edom is the enemy of God and of Israel.

'You can read in Ezekiel 25:12–14 and Isaiah 34, where it says that Edom is the symbol for the enemy of God. In Amos 1:11–12 we read how Edom is persecuting his brother with only one goal, his destruction. In Malachi 1:2–5 Edom is called the Land of Godlessness, the people the Lord God hates for ever. And in Jeremiah 49:7–22 we read about God's judgement on Edom. Perhaps the most important chapter is Isaiah 63, where the Messiah himself brings judgement over Edom. Here we also read how, when bringing judgement over Edom, the Messiah is wondering why no one stood with him against Edom, because in Isaiah 63:5 it says "I looked, but there was no one to help . . . so my arm worked salvation for me, and my own wrath sustained me." Edom is a spirit who hates God and will try to destroy the way of salvation in two ways:

1. By destroying the nation of Israel.
2. By destroying the believing church.

'How does this spirit of Edom get hold of nations and people? Just as he did with Ishmael, through feelings of inferiority. As well as it being a driving spirit of Islam, I believe this spirit of Edom gets hold of individual men and nations through feelings of inferiority.

'Inferiority is a universal feeling. Since the Fall, many have struggled with inferiority. Sometimes we don't know who we are. Sometimes we don't know who God is. When we don't know who we are we can lose our self-worth.

'When a nation or individual people are struggling for worth and acceptance, it's offensive to them when they hear of a nation that calls itself elected by God, loved by God and chosen by God. This gives birth to jealousy in people and nations. People are not able to agree with this. They get angry and this jealousy drives them to hate those who are chosen.

'This can even happen to Christian believers if they have not properly understood what the Messiah has given them, that God has nothing more to give than his Son. There is nothing more precious than the blood of the Messiah. Those who have not understood this will always have problems because they still think that maybe the Jewish people have something more than they have. These believers have not been delivered from this feeling of inferiority. They do not understand what it means to be a child of God.

'In the fourth century, Christians started to persecute Jews when they lost sight of their identity and their relationship to Israel and they began to replace the Jewish people in their calling by saying the church had replaced Israel as God's chosen people.

'Islam, too, is a replacement religion. It wants to replace the calling of the Jewish people: something Islam learnt from the church. Before Islam existed officially as a religion, some of the early church fathers were teaching Replacement Theology and saying that God had finished with the Jewish people. They taught that the Jewish people had failed because they rejected the Messiah, so God had abandoned them, and they started to persecute the Jews.

'When Muhammad started to found Islam, he was a man who was searching for an answer for his own people. He met Jews and Christians and he saw that they had Holy Scriptures, whereas the Arab tribes didn't – they believed in different gods and had many idols. Muhammad realised this would destroy the Arabs unless they got a revelation from the God of the Jews and the Christians. The Koran describes how Muhammad started to get "revelations". But the kind of revelations he got were driving him to commit suicide. Muhammad, however, had a clever wife who gave him confidence and persuaded him not to give up. Muhammad started to preach to his community. But they did not like what he was preaching and started to persecute him, so he went to Ethiopia where he was cared for by some Christians. Without the church, he would not have survived.

'Eventually he went back to his own people. In Medina, a city not far from Mecca, they had a problem: unrest and violence were somehow destroying the whole city. Muhammad saw his opportunity. He was a statesman, he realised he was able to solve this problem and started to teach his so-called revelation. And so it was that the first Islamic community came into beginning. Islam means "the one who bows under God's law and authority".

'Now Muhammad always thought that what he believed and taught was the same as what Jews and Christians believed and taught. In the beginning he even said to his disciples "Go to the Jews and Christians, they will confirm that what I teach is the truth because that is what they believe." He wanted to be accepted as a prophet by the Jews, and in Medina at that time there were almost forty thousand Jews living. However, the Jews did not accept Muhammad. They said "How can you be a prophet? You are not a Jew, you do not know the Scriptures, how can we accept you?" This experience of being rejected by the Jews hurt Muhammad deeply and the spirit of Edom was able to take hold of him.

'And so it was that he established Islam in a way that was independent of the Jews and the Christians. He did it very cleverly. He said that Abraham, his forefather, was not a Jew and he was not a Christian, because the Jews are since Sinai, and the Christians are since Christ; so all the fathers before that, Isaac, Jacob etc, were not Jews because Judaism didn't exist at that time. The law had not been given. There was no Torah, so there was no Judaism. If Abraham is not a Jew or a Christian, what is he? He is one who bows under God's authority; therefore he is a Muslim. When God tried to bring the message of Islam to the world he chose the Jews first but they failed because they persecuted and killed the prophets. That's why God has rejected them and given them over to be judged by the only righteous community, the Islamic community. The Christians too have failed. They called the Messiah, who was only a prophet, God. So the only religion that is not corrupted, the only religion that is pure, is Islam, and God had called him to proclaim the pure message of God.

'You can read in the Koran that Islam is the religion that believes it is superior over all other religions and so must rule over the nations. That's why Islam talks about "two houses". One house is called the "House of Islam" or the "House of Peace"; the other house is called the "House of War". Included in the House of Islam are the parts of the world that live under Islamic law, while the House of War represents the rest of the world that is not yet under Islamic law. Muhammad understood himself to be the one who was called to bring the whole world back under the law of Islam. The aim of Islam is to conquer every place of power, including Jerusalem, in order to take back the inheritance, the spiritual inheritance and the land.

'It was significant that eighteen years after Islam was founded, Muslims conquered Jerusalem. A lot of people ask today, why do the Muslims claim Jerusalem, when it is not mentioned in the Koran?

'We have to understand that Jerusalem is the only city that is called by Islam the "holy one". Al-Quds, its Arabic name, means "the holy one". So Jerusalem is the most important city to Muslims. The first Muslims, when they prayed, looked towards Jerusalem, not Mecca. That they later turned towards Mecca was a political move by Muhammad because he wanted to conquer Mecca. In

Islamic tradition Jerusalem is the city where the last judgement will take place. Jerusalem is the city where the angel will come down on the Temple Mount and blow the trumpet to open up the final judgement. Jerusalem is understood in Islamic tradition as the gate to heaven. Muslims consider the Temple Mount or Mount Moriah the "place of power" and the one who rules over this place has the spiritual authority.

'So Jerusalem is no ordinary city for Islam. The aim of every Islamic movement in the world is to deliver Jerusalem from the enemy. Why? Because Jerusalem is the place of struggle over the inheritance.

'When the Jewish people returned to Israel, and particularly after 1967, when they recaptured the Temple Mount, Islam felt deeply threatened. Whilst Islam ruled over Jerusalem, which it did for 1,300 years, Muslims did not feel challenged. We should not forget that until fifty years go, the church knew hardly anything about Islam. It took the establishment of the state of Israel to expose the reality of Islam. As God put his hand on this land through the Jewish people, Islam started to manifest. Today everybody knows something about Islam. They know the violent character of Islam. They know its determination to destroy this nation.

'When I talk about Islam I don't mean the entire Arab population of the world. The Arabs and Muslims are not more evil than we are. They are human beings just like the Jews and Americans, the British and the Swiss, who are in need of salvation. We have to understand that our fight is not against flesh and blood. We don't hate the Arabs as people: how can we? If we believe in the Messiah, how can we hate people? But we are engaged in a spiritual fight and the enemy is utilising people. He has poisoned their thinking and imprisoned their minds for two reasons:

1. To destroy Israel.
2. To destroy people.

'Islam, the spirit of Edom, wants to destroy, no matter whom. Its hatred against God manifests itself in hatred against Israel and against God's creation. I really believe that God is deeply saddened by the death of every Jew and every Arab. That's why we have to understand this demonic system of Islam and start to pray that God will deliver the Arab nations out of it. But we also have to understand that there is not a humanistic solution to the conflict we are in. Compromise over the land will not solve the problem because this is not a fight between people; it's a fight between the spirits.

'Why has God committed himself to restore Israel? In Ezekiel 36 the Lord gives his reason very clearly. He says "I will give you a new heart and put a new spirit in you." Why? "Then the nations will know that I am the Lord, when I show myself holy through you before their eyes."

'We have to understand that Israel did not come into being as a result of the UN or as a result of the guilty conscience of Europe. Israel came into being because God said "I will gather you from all the countries and bring you back into your own land . . . you will be my people and I will be your God" (Ezek. 36:24, 28).

'Today we are witnesses of God's fulfilment of his promises. And many in the church thought God had given up on Israel.

'So God's plan is that he wants the nations to know that he is the Lord. And they will know this, he says, "when I show myself holy through you (Israel) before their eyes".

'How, then, should we pray? Don't waste time praying for a human compromise. I believe God is going to give the Palestinians life. I do not believe in a God who excludes. I believe that God wants to give to the Arabs and Palestinians, even in this land, a place to live and to prosper; but on his conditions, not on their conditions or on the conditions of the government of Israel, or on the conditions of the Americans.

'God says "If my people, who are called by my name, will humble themselves and pray and seek my face and turn from their wicked ways, then will I hear from heaven and will forgive their sin and will heal their land" (2 Chr. 7:14).

'The Scriptures are very clear that this land is God's land and even Israel has to be very careful. History shows us that the Lord has cast Israel out of this land several times because of her behaviour.

'Today we are looking forward to a time when this nation of Israel, the Jewish people, will be a place of blessing for the nations, not a place of curse. At the same time we can see that Islam tries to use the Arab nations and the Palestinians to hinder God's restoration of the nation of Israel. I do not believe in a Palestinian state, not because I don't love the Palestinians but for quite the opposite reason: because I love them I don't wish them a Palestinian state because it's not in God's plan, and anything that is not in God's plan is a curse. I pray with all my heart that God will deliver the Palestinians from this Islamic system that is trying to destroy them.

'So when you pray, pray for three things:

1. That God will break and humiliate the system of Islam in order to release and to save the Arab nations who are imprisoned in this system. Arabs will always hate Israel while this spirit imprisons them. Islam will never give up until all Israel is destroyed.

2. Pray for the church, that this time it will stand with the Messiah in recognising the spirit of Islam and stand against the spirit but for the people, so that the Lord will not say again "I was looking around when I dealt with Edom and no one stood with me." We should not forget that the spirit of Edom has imprisoned almost one-and-a-half billion people.

3. Pray for the Israeli government, that God will give them revelation so that they will not bow before the nations who want to force them to compromise. It is very difficult for the government because they too deal with a reality that is bigger than they are and their wisdom is not enough to solve this problem. Pray for the government, that God will raise up people who understand the inheritance of Israel and start to call upon the only one who is able to solve this conflict, to bring security and restoration to Israel and salvation and life to the Arabs.'

Contact details for COR (correspondence will be forwarded to Marcel Rebiai or the COR office in Jerusalem):
Head office in Switzerland:
GDV COR
PO Box 77
8625 Gossau / ZH
Switzerland

Tel: 41 1 935 47 51
Fax: 41 1 936 14 00
Email: sekretariat@gdv-cor.org

CHAPTER 6

LIFE FROM THE DEAD

By R.T. Kendall

'For if their rejection is the reconciliation of the world, what will their acceptance be but life from the dead?' (Rom. 11:15)

'Yasser Arafat will see you tomorrow evening at six o'clock', said the voice on the other end of the telephone. I received this call at my hotel in Tiberias on 2 July 2002. The voice was that of Revd Andrew White, Canon of Coventry Cathedral and the Archbishop of Canterbury's special envoy to the Middle East. With me were Alan Bell and Lyndon Bowring, who had flown into Israel a day or two before in order to spend some time with me, relaxing and swimming in the Sea of Galilee. We were hardly prepared for this surprising development.

And yet I should not have been so surprised, considering the events that led up to that moment. 'Who despises the day of small things?' (Zech. 4:10). The day of small things in this case included two prophetic words given to me, neither of which I took as seriously as I should have. Both of these prophecies – from two different people – related directly to trips I would be making to Israel.

This chapter is largely about prophecy. There are essentially three kinds of prophecy. The first is prophecy in Holy Scripture – infallible and unchanging – that sometimes points to the future, especially the last days. When we speak of eschatology (the doctrine of 'last things'), we are referring to prophecy in the Bible, as in Daniel, the teachings of Jesus and the book of Revelation – but also the letters of Paul, as in Romans 11 and other places.

The second kind of prophecy is preaching. We who are preachers are given a mandate to speak as if our words were the very words of God (1 Pet. 4:11). Such preaching of course must be tested and never regarded as infallible (Rom. 12:3–6).

There is a third kind of prophecy and it is always secondary – and probably third – in importance. This level should not be regarded as infallible even if there are examples when the word was given by someone who previously got it exactly right. For the person prophesying might get it wrong next time! Such prophecy therefore must always be tested, as Paul states in 1 Thessalonians 5:21. This is when a person gives a prophetic word to another individual or to a church. When Paul hoped all Corinthians would prophesy (1 Cor. 14:1ff), he was referring to one of the gifts of the Holy Spirit mentioned in 1 Corinthians 12:8–10, namely the gift of prophecy. But the words that flow from this level of prophecy must, as in preaching, always be subservient to Holy Scripture. One should never *equate* this level of prophecy with Holy Scripture. And yet Paul did urge that we must never despise or underestimate someone prophesying to us (1 Thess. 5:20).

In October of 2001, a month before I planned to go to Israel for the first time with Lyndon and Alan, John Paul Jackson told me emphatically that something would happen on that trip that would be the beginning of something very significant, and that I would always look back on that trip as the time it began. John Paul had prophesied to me before and so far had got it right every time, but I queried this one because my trip to Israel was merely to be a week of 'down time' with these special friends. In fact it was designed entirely as a final farewell. Our retirement was set for some two months later and these very special friends wanted to say goodbye to me in a memorable way. It was memorable indeed – so much so that all we could think about after that was how we could do it again! But we assumed it was a time that could not be repeated.

I had agreed a year before to help lead a Holy Land tour in June 2002. This tour was sponsored by Premier Radio, and Julia Fisher was one of the organizers. When we retired from Westminster Chapel I promised Julia that I would fly back in order to join her, Bishop John Taylor and Rob Frost, who were also leaders of the tour. But I really thought it would be cancelled. For one thing, there was hope that five thousand would come on the tour to fulfil a wish expressed by Martin Luther King that five thousand Christians would gather on the Mount of Beatitudes to pray for peace in Israel. This was the inspiration that originally lay behind the tour. Only 250 signed up, and with the suicide bombings happening every week I was convinced it would be cancelled. In the meantime, Lyndon and Alan came up with the idea to 'do it again' if indeed the tour was not cancelled, and join me in Israel once the tour was over and the 250 Brits had gone back to the UK. I thought this was lovely but still did not expect it to come off.

I come now to the second prophetic word to which I referred above. I was sitting in Snapper's restaurant with some friends in Key Largo, Florida, where Louise and I now live. A man I had just met named Don Vinson asked me, referring to my preaching schedule, 'Where are you going next?' 'Oh,' I replied, 'it looks like I will have to go to Israel next week.' As soon as I spoke he looked at me and said calmly 'Something of great significance will happen while you are over there, beyond what you think you are going to Israel for, and the significance is for Israel.' I looked at him with a shrug of my shoulders. In the parking lot he repeated this to my friend Randy Wall as I headed for my car: 'R.T. will find he is going there for a reason beyond what he thinks he is going there for.' His friend David Rhea actually 'manifested' when hearing these words – his body shook, and both of them nearly fell to the ground in a puddle of water in the parking lot. Don Vinson explained to me that he felt the Spirit of God come on him in power the moment I said I was going to Israel and that he 'went into intercession' as he repeated this to Randy Wall. I am almost ashamed to say that when I looked at my journal (which I have kept daily for years – in detail) for that evening, I don't even mention Don Vinson's name or word, only that I 'went to Snapper's with some friends'. 'Who despises the day of small things?' I'm afraid I did.

I pray for Osama bin Laden every day

On 23 June 2002 I arrived in Tel Aviv. As I came out of customs there was a man with a sign saying 'Dr Kendall', so I introduced myself. He was an Arab, a Palestinian, and had been asked to drive me to my hotel in Jerusalem. He opened the back door but I asked if I could sit up front with him if only because I love the ride to Jerusalem.

'What's your name?' I asked.

'Osama,' he replied with a smile, knowing I would pick up on the famous name.

'Listen to me,' I said. 'I pray for Osama bin Laden every day.'

'You do? Why?' he asked incredulously.

'That God will touch his heart.'

'Oh, I see,' Osama replied.

'Have you any idea what it would mean if Osama bin Laden were converted to Jesus Christ?'

'I hadn't thought of that but I see what you mean,' he replied.

I told him about John Wesley, who used to say that God does nothing but in answer to prayer. 'If that's true, somebody must have been praying for Saul of Tarsus, the greatest terrorist alive at the time, and look at what happened. I even pray for Yasser Arafat.'

'You pray for Yasser Arafat?' he replied with some amazement. I told him that I began doing this in 1982 because Arthur Blessitt, a man who has carried a cross around the world, told me certain things that Arafat had told him which made me want to start praying for Arafat.

'What would you say if you met Yasser Arafat?' he asked.

I said I would ask to pray with him.

'What would you say in your prayer?'

I replied that Arafat needs a lot of wisdom at the moment and I would pray that God would give him wisdom. President George W. Bush had said only days before that Arafat should be replaced, so he clearly needs a lot of wisdom.

'Would you like to meet Arafat?'

'Of course I would.' My mind went back to Don Vinson's word to me in Snapper's. Osama picked up his mobile phone and started calling people he knew. The problem was, despite the fact that my Arab driver turned out to be well connected, the Israeli government would not let anybody into Ramallah at the present time – absolutely nobody. We drove up to our hotel in Jerusalem and he said he would keep trying to get me into Ramallah and that he would love to take me there himself.

I ran into Julia Fisher in the hotel lobby and told her about my conversation with Osama. She later introduced me to the Bishop of Jerusalem – a Palestinian – to see if he could get me into Ramallah to meet Arafat. And yet, even though nobody is better connected to influential people than he is, sadly he had to say that since President Bush had said those things about Arafat the Israeli government had decided to clamp down and let nobody – including Western journalists – into Ramallah. So it was all out of the question. 'Oh well,' I thought. I hadn't come to Israel to meet Yasser Arafat anyway, so the idea was put to one side.

On the evening of 26 June I was invited to speak in the Dormitian Abbey, a church situated on Mount Zion and very near the spot, it is believed, where the Holy Spirit came down on the day of Pentecost. It was a great honour, but somehow I had not read the literature handed out to everyone on the tour and did not know until the day itself that I was to address the entire group of 250 that night besides invited people from all over Jerusalem, including church and religious leaders. It was billed as one of the highlights of the tour. The All Souls orchestra and chorus, led by Noel Tredinnick, would give a concert and I would bring the evening to a close with a twenty-minute address. Since the purpose of the tour was to pray for peace, I thought I could use an old sermon on the subject of prayer that would be appropriate.

But something rather extraordinary happened only an hour or so before this service. Thoughts began to pour into my mind and heart that were altogether different from a sermon on praying for the peace of Jerusalem. I felt a burning in my heart like I had not experienced in a long time. Thoughts I never dreamed of poured into me. I wrote as fast as I could and came up with a fresh word for the meeting at the Dormitian Abbey. I have prepared and preached sermons since 1954 and I know when the anointing comes and when it doesn't. It came. Totally unexpectedly. These thoughts will occupy much of this chapter.

Some of us wished the evening had been tape-recorded, most certainly the concert. The All Souls orchestra and chorus were brilliant. What a pity it was not recorded, because the acoustics were fantastic. But my message somehow – to God be all the praise – made an impact that nobody, including me, expected. The atmosphere was electric. I returned to my hotel to phone Louise to say I had just experienced one of the greatest nights of my whole life. I recalled Don Vinson's word at Snapper's and wondered if there might be something to his word to me after all. I was amazed at things I was given to say and thrilled to see how my words were received. But, alas, not by all. The people on the tour, however, were delighted and many came up to me to say 'We have wondered why somebody doesn't say these things – and we are so glad you did.'

Had my talk been recorded I could simply have it typed out to form part of this chapter. But I must refer to the notes I used that evening at the Dormitian Abbey and try to recall what I said, although I intend to enlarge on some of the points. I believe they are relevant for the church, the nation of Israel, Jews generally, and even people in the Islamic world as well.

I announced as my subject 'What if you had only five minutes to speak to the people of Israel: what would you say?' In other words, if you had only five minutes to address the Knesset (the Israeli parliament), to speak to the nation of Israel on television – or just to talk to one Israeli at a time, for five minutes, and you had to make every word count, what exactly would you say? This question certainly challenged me, and sobered me; I felt, however, it was one I myself should have an answer for. In my talk at the Dormitian Abbey I suggested three things, once I introduced the subject. These three points could probably be stated in five minutes and, in my opinion, be stated with effectiveness, most certainly if the Holy Spirit applied the words to the hearers. For this, I believe, is exactly what the people of Israel need to hear. It is my dream that these three items could be addressed one day in Israel. If Martin Luther King's wish were to be fulfilled and the prayers of five thousand people actually answered, what follows is the way – and, in my opinion, the only way – that peace will come to the area known as the Holy Land.

The way forward for peace in Israel generally and Jerusalem in particular, then, is theological. Not political or through a military solution. It is a biblical mandate to pray for the peace of Jerusalem. When I was minister of Westminster Chapel I prayed publicly every Sunday for peace in the Middle East and for the peace of Jerusalem. When David three thousand years ago penned Psalm 122, which includes the plea 'Pray for the peace of Jerusalem' (v. 6), he could not have known how relevant those words would be in the early part of the twenty-first century. But they are. This prayer is needed today more than ever. The threat to Jerusalem's security in 1000 BC was a drop in the bucket compared to the need for its security at the present time.

The ancient city of Jerusalem, especially the Temple Mount, is regarded as holy and special to Christians, Jews and Muslims. All three religions could articulate cogent reasons why this area is special. You can be sure that neither Muslims nor many Israelis (those who are Orthodox in particular) are ready to turn over the Temple Mount to the other. A few fundamentalist Christians even think that the temple must be rebuilt and sometimes get as emotionally involved in the issue as some Orthodox Jews and religious Palestinians. None of these three groups is happy that it be an 'international' place; each of these feels strongly it belongs to them and no one else and will not give up claiming this area until it is firmly their own.

I will not address the issue of who has the true legal right to the Holy Land generally and Jerusalem in particular. Even if it were proved biblically beyond any doubt that this land belongs to Israel and Jews, not to Arabs or Palestinians, the fight for the Temple Mount would continue. Islamic people will stick to the Koran while Jews and Christians appeal to the Old and New Testament. No international forum would have real authority in any case and the United Nations will never take sides with the Bible or the Koran.

The thesis of this chapter (this being the thrust of my talk at the Dormitian Abbey) can be stated as follows. Lofty and noble – and biblical – though praying for the peace of Jerusalem is, there is a greater and higher goal: to pray with all our hearts for the salvation of Israelis and Jews and for the lifting of the blindness that is on both of them and the Islamic world to the glory of Jesus Christ. Paul summed it up: 'The god of this age [Satan] has blinded the minds of unbelievers, so that they cannot see the light of the gospel of the glory of Christ, who is the image of God' (2 Cor. 4:4). The Jews generally have not accepted Jesus Christ as their Lord and Messiah because they have been blinded to the glory of Christ by the devil. The same is true of the Islamic people. However much good people may say they admire Jesus, they will not bow to his Deity or confess him as the Saviour who shed his blood on the cross for our sins. This is what must be preached. Nothing else will do. Nothing else will bring peace to Jerusalem.

I made this very statement on a Christian television programme recently and the minister who interviewed me interrupted: 'Yes, but this cannot happen until the Second Coming of Jesus.' Wrong. It will happen before then! It is my view that we must pray that the way be found for this message to be brought to the Israelis, most of whom have not even read the Old Testament, let alone heard the gospel. At the moment it is extremely difficult to spread the gospel in Israel. Missionaries are not allowed in and it is dangerous for anybody to be seen or heard preaching this gospel to an Israeli citizen. This is what lay behind my question regarding having five minutes to speak to the people.

'For if their rejection is the reconciliation of the world, what will their acceptance be but life from the dead?'

The verse quoted at the beginning of this chapter must be examined: 'For if their rejection is the reconciliation of the world, what will their acceptance be but life from the dead?' (Rom. 11:15). This verse indicates four things:

1. *Rejection.* This, sadly, is the clearest word that can be used to describe the reaction of Jews generally to the person and good news of Jesus Christ. Isaiah saw it coming many years in advance: 'Who has believed our message and to whom has the arm of the Lord been revealed? . . . He was despised and rejected by men, a man of sorrows, and familiar with suffering. Like one from whom men hide their faces he was despised, and we esteemed him not. Surely he took up our infirmities and carried our sorrows, yet we considered him stricken by God, smitten by him, and afflicted. . . . We all, like sheep, have gone astray, and each of us has turned to his own way; and the Lord has laid on him the iniquity of us all. . . . he was cut off from the land of the living; for the transgression of my people he was stricken' (Is. 53:1–8).

Writing in Ephesus many years after Jesus died, John, one of the original twelve disciples, summed up Jesus' success (if one dare use this word) in this manner: 'He came to that which was his own, but his own did not receive him' (Jn. 1:11). I wish with all my heart they had never said it, but the Jews demanded that Pilate execute him and even said 'Let his blood be on us and on our children' (Mt. 27:25). They fulfilled Isaiah's prophecy in this. They were so sure that God himself was punishing Jesus for blasphemy that they were convinced they were in God's will and that Jesus was stricken and smitten by God himself. They were not the slightest bit worried about their words at the time.

Before his crucifixion, Jesus gave a parable that forecast the events which included his own rejection by the Jews and his being accepted by Gentiles instead (Mt. 21:33–42). Jesus then made an application: 'Therefore I tell you that the kingdom of God will be taken away from you [the Jews] and given to a people [the Gentiles] who will produce its fruit' (Mt. 21:43). This was borne out by his being crucified by his own people, but also by the small numbers of Jews who actually did receive the gospel after the Holy Spirit fell on the church. Yes, there were three thousand converted on the day of Pentecost (Acts 2:41) and the numbers increased to five thousand later (Acts 4:4). But this was a small percentage of Jews. Moreover, wherever the Apostle Paul went, the pattern became predictable: the Jews rejected him and he turned to Gentiles (e.g. Acts 13:46; 18:6).

2. *Reconciliation*. When Paul referred to the reconciliation of the world in Romans 11:15 he did not mean that all Gentiles were saved or would be saved. Indeed, Paul made this clear in 2 Corinthians 5 when he said that God was in Christ reconciling the world to himself but immediately added that we must preach: 'We implore you on Christ's behalf: Be reconciled to God' (vv. 19–20). What Paul means by reconciliation of the world, then, refers to the fact that Christ died for Gentiles as well as for Jews (2 Cor. 5:14–15). But Gentiles still need to hear the gospel and respond positively to it or they will be eternally lost.

What happened was this. A spiritual blindness came upon the people of Israel generally after Jews rejected their Messiah. This did not mean that a Jew could not be saved. But it implied that a Jew being converted to Jesus Christ would be an exceedingly rare event. You could say that a 'double blindness' is on Israel. All people are afflicted with this blindness to the glory of Christ (2 Cor. 4:4). But for Paul to speak of a separate kind of blindness where Israel is concerned suggests they were given a double dose of blindness as a punishment for turning their backs on his one and only Son. Paul quotes from Deuteronomy 29:4: 'God gave them a spirit of stupor, eyes so that they could not see and ears so that they could not hear, to this very day' (Rom. 11:8).

But, strange though it seems, Israel's rejection of the gospel was ironically the means by which Gentiles were offered covenant privileges that had always been exclusive to the Jews. Jews are depicted as a natural olive tree,

Gentiles as a 'wild' olive tree that has been 'grafted in' (Rom. 11:16–18). We who are Gentiles, then, get in on what was the privilege of Jews only. They are God's natural olive tree. Like it or not, Jews are special to God. He has always had a 'soft spot' for Israel. But he was very angry when they rejected that which was on offer to them first of all. This anger was manifested in two ways: (1) Jews being inflicted with blindness to the gospel and (2) the Gentiles being made ready to receive what the Jews didn't want. Jews are God's covenant people because they are born Jews. This gives them certain advantages over all others (Rom. 3:1–2). But this does not make them regenerate (born again). It never has and never will – any more than you or I, if born into a Christian home, would automatically be born again because of our parentage. We still need to hear and receive the gospel or we will be forever lost.

So too the Jews. Never, never, never think that all Jews will go to heaven when they die – or that each individual Jew will be given a second chance after death – just because they are Jews. They must be saved by faith in the blood of Christ. And if they die unregenerate they will be eternally lost as much as a Gentile who is unsaved. There is not one shred of evidence in Scripture that Jews will be given a second chance. They must believe the gospel while they are alive or be lost when they die. No second chance. I wish it were not true, but all Jews who have been born over the last two thousand years are given no hope whatever of salvation if they did not believe the gospel first. This is the case with Gentiles. This is the case with Jews.

And yet their rejection of Jesus has meant that Gentiles have been given a wonderful privilege. This is good news to Gentiles like me – and also to all Muslims. The gospel is offered to Muslims and they – a part of what is called a wild olive tree – can get in on what were once exclusive covenant privileges for Jews only. If you say to me that this special affection God has long had for Israel will turn off Islamic people and will alienate them from Jesus, I answer: you will never convert anybody apart from the truth. Muslims who turn to Jesus Christ must, sooner or later, admit they have been privileged – as I a Gentile have been – to be grafted into the natural olive tree. A Muslim will probably never be converted on the basis of theological argument. It will be love from our hearts that will do it, if anything. As the poem goes:

> 'Twas not the truth you taught, to you so clear, to me so dim;
> But when you came to me, you brought a sense of him;
> Yes, from your eyes he beckoned me, from your heart his
> love was shed,
> And I lost sight of you and saw the Christ instead.
>
> (Author unknown)

Gentiles, then, whether sons and daughters of Ishmael, Brits or Americans, are fortunate to have the gospel given to them at all, not to mention to have their eyes opened by God's sheer grace and be saved. Early Gentiles were thrilled at this. 'When the Gentiles heard this, they were glad and honoured the word of the Lord; and all who were appointed for eternal life believed' (Acts 13:48). Those who were appointed – meaning sovereign election by grace – were the beneficiaries of eternal life. Therefore it is not enough to be a Gentile to be saved; you must receive the gospel. Those who do so are called God's elect – whether Jew or Gentile. You can be a Jew and not be one of God's elect; you can be a Gentile and not be one of God's elect. You can, however, be a Jew and be one of God's elect (if you receive the gospel) and you can be a Gentile and be one of God's elect (if you receive the gospel). But because Jews generally rejected the gospel originally offered to them, God turned to a non-Jewish world in order to make up a bride for his Son. Paul calls this the reconciliation of the world in Romans 11:15.

3. *Receiving*. This is what Paul means by 'acceptance' – accepting, or receiving, the gospel they once rejected. Paul is talking about Jews receiving Jesus. This part of Romans 11:15 refers partly to an individual Jew receiving the Lord Jesus Christ, but mainly to Jews receiving him in mass numbers. Therefore Paul is speaking partly to show that a Jew can be saved and be a glorious exception to the rule; but he is mostly speaking prophetically in his anticipation that one day there will be a turning of Jews *en masse* to Jesus Christ before his Second Coming. Paul is thus speaking eschatologically much of the time in Romans 11.

In Romans 9 he laments that his brothers, those of his own race, have generally rejected the gospel. 'I have great sorrow and unceasing anguish in my heart. For I could wish that I myself were cursed and cut off from Christ for the sake of my brothers, those of my own race, the people of Israel' (Rom. 9:2–4). He then goes on to show that God's elect – those who have been chosen – are granted saving faith not because of being born into a particular race. 'For not all who are descended from Israel are Israel. Nor because they are his descendants are they all Abraham's children' (Rom. 9:6–7). God is not limited to the people who make up the natural olive tree to find his elect. He is sovereign, has always been so, and said to Moses 'I will have mercy on whom I have mercy, and I will have compassion on whom I have compassion' (Rom. 9:15). His elect, therefore, are made up from Gentiles as well as Jews. This is nothing new, says Paul. Hosea saw it in advance: 'I will call them [Gentiles] "my people" who are not my people [Jews]' (Rom. 9:25). Therefore the rejection of the gospel by the Jews did not take God by surprise, neither was his offering of the privileges of the covenant to Gentiles a last-minute decision.

In Romans 10 Paul gives the reason why the Jews rejected Jesus. They 'sought to establish their own' right-eousness (and yet this is the reason everyone else as well rejects the gospel). They would not submit to the right-eousness of God (Rom. 10:3). They have a zeal for God, yes, but it is not based on knowledge, namely the knowl-edge of the gospel. In Romans 3:9 Paul declared in one stroke that both Jews and Gentiles are alike 'under sin' – which means they are all lost and need to be saved or they will go to hell when they die. Paul thus gives the condi-tions for salvation in Romans 10:9: 'If [a very big "if"] you confess with your mouth, "Jesus is Lord," and believe in your heart that God raised him from the dead, you will be saved.' This is the condition for salvation, whether you are Jew or Gentile. Those who confess Jesus as Lord and believe he was raised from the dead are saved; all others are not. Paul then added that Isaiah too saw in advance that Gentiles would be let in on covenant privileges: 'I was found by those [Gentiles] who did not seek me; I revealed myself to those who did not ask for me' (Rom. 10:20). We who are Gentiles, therefore, did nothing what-ever to cause God to turn to us. Nothing. It was by grace alone. Gentiles who confess Jesus as Lord and believe in his resurrection from the dead are treated with the same privileges as a Jew would have been given, had that Jew confessed the same. Now that might suggest that God has finished with the natural seed of Abraham and has given up entirely on Jews.

Paul therefore anticipates a question, that is, if you have followed him up to this point. If you think to ask this question, it shows you have understood him; if it has not occurred to you to ask this question, go back and re-read what he has just said! The question is, 'Did God reject his people?' (Rom. 11:l). In other words, did the Jews' rejection of his Son anger him so much that he categorically rejected them as a 'tit for tat' kind of retribution? No, not at all, he insists. The first proof of this is that Paul himself is from the tribe of Benjamin. That is sufficient proof that being a Jew does not mean you cannot be saved. For Paul, a Jew, was saved. But he adds: those he did not reject are those he 'foreknew' (Rom. 11:2). So we are back to sovereign election again. Paul implicitly says that he himself is one of God's chosen. He then refers to Elijah. Why bring up Elijah? Because any Hebrew Christian at this point might fall into the 'Elijah complex', the notion that he was the only one who served God, that he alone was left. But Elijah soon learned that he wasn't the only one – there were no fewer than seven thousand who had Elijah's faith (Rom. 11:4). So don't be surprised, says Paul, that there are Jews being converted now and then. Maybe not in great numbers, but there will be some and perhaps far more than one might think. Therefore Paul draws a conclusion: 'At the present time there is a remnant chosen by grace' (Rom. 11:5). But who might that remnant be? Would that remnant be Jews only? No. There would be non-Jews who are chosen by grace.

Paul then puts an astonishing distinction between Israel and the elect. In case someone hastily assumed that Israel and the elect are always the same, that somebody might refer to 'Israel' and 'elect' synonymously, he pauses to show what may be hard for many to swallow: that they are not necessarily the same! Indeed, 'What Israel sought so earnestly [by its zeal for God] it did not obtain [salvation], but the elect [those God chose from Jews and Gentiles] did' (Rom. 11:7). This shows again, as he showed in Romans 10:3, that the Jews thought they would be saved by their righteousness – but missed salvation altogether. But not to worry, says Paul, God has an elect and you can be sure that the elect will be saved. This is because the elect are not chosen from the natural seed of Abraham alone. In a word: God's elect are made up of Jews and Gentiles he sovereignly chose.

But that is not the end of the story. For the question that has puzzled and sometimes divided many good Christians for a long time is this. Does God's elect, though chosen from Jews and Gentiles, become the substitute, or replacement, for ancient Israel? In other words, does 'Israel' take on a new meaning, or definition – like 'spiritual Israel' or, simply, the church? This would mean that there is no longer an Israel – as it has always been known – in God's sight or ours. This would mean that what we always thought of as Israel simply ended at some stage, presumably when Israel as a whole rejected the Messiah promised to them. If this is so, Israel – as we have known it – no longer exists. We could only speak of the church, God's elect people or 'spiritual' Israel. Is that Paul's teaching?

I answer, no. Paul's question in Romans 11:1, 'Did God reject his people?' – the answer to which was 'by no means!' – not only paved the way for a Jew being saved, as Paul was, but paved the way for the very questions I just raised in the previous paragraph. We could pose the question like this and get Paul's meaning: did God reject his people and replace them with a different word – the church? Since Paul grants that the elect comprise both Jews and Gentiles, one might wonder if God did indeed reject his ancient people called Israel and now regards his people as simply believers in Jesus. But the original question 'Did God reject his people?' – meaning Israel – and answering that question with a categorical 'no' was *intended to show* that the church, or God's elect, did not render Israel non-existent in his eyes. It is true the church, or God's elect, is what may rightly be called 'spiritual Israel' in the same way that every Gentile believer also may be called a Jew – since he is 'inwardly' a Jew, by 'circumcision of the heart, by the Spirit' (Rom. 2:29). But that does not mean there are no more Jews and that there is no more Israel. They most certainly do exist.

So with this in mind Paul asked the question yet again: 'Did they [Israel] stumble [by rejecting their Messiah] so as to fall beyond recovery [cease to exist]?' The answer is the same: 'Not at all!' (Rom. 11:11). And if there were any doubt about that, Paul hoped that the conversion of Gentiles would even make Jews jealous! 'Salvation has come to the Gentiles to make Israel envious.' (Rom. 11:11) The only Israel that could be meant is, simply, ancient Israel. That means Israel continued to exist as he wrote Romans 11. He hoped that the conversion of Gentiles would have the effect of making Jews want to turn to Jesus Christ after all. If that were to happen, he continues, the consequence would be incalculable. The verse that heads the chapter of this book – Romans 11:15 – is anticipated in verse 12: 'But if their transgression [Israel's sin in rejecting Jesus] means riches for the world [the offer of the gospel to Gentiles], how much greater riches will their fullness bring! [coming into their true identity by embracing Jesus].'

Two things in particular emerge in these lines that will bear mentioning: (1) Paul at best only expects to save 'some' Jews (Rom. 11:14) at the moment, but (2) he expects this to change so that at some point in the future there will be a mass turning of the Jews to the Lord Jesus Christ. Whether he expected to see this in his own day is not clear, but it seems unlikely since he later talks about this happening only after 'the full number of the Gentiles has come in' (Rom. 11:25). It was in the future then and it is in the future now – but perhaps not much longer!

4. *Resurrection*. This is why he states this key verse: 'For if their rejection [of the gospel] is the reconciliation of the world [the offer of the gospel to Gentiles], what will their acceptance [of the gospel] be but life from the dead?' (Rom. 11:15).

'Life from the dead' – the phrase he uses to describe a turning of Israel en masse to Christ – is exactly what he expects at some stage in the future. This is why I said above that he is speaking prophetically. It is something he believes will happen. And since I am committed to the infallibility of Scripture, I take this to mean that it will indeed happen!

In what sense is a mass acceptance of the gospel by Israel to be 'life from the dead'? First, it would be a mir-acle – it would defy a natural explanation – to see hun-dreds of thousands of Jews all over the world, and Israelis in particular, suddenly turn to Jesus. Second, as Jesus promised his own resurrection but few believed it, so this lifting of the blindness on Israel is promised. Indeed, says Paul, 'God is able to graft them in again' (Rom. 11:23) – a word he would not put in writing if God had not already predestined it. Third, the excitement, awe and fear it would bring all over the world are beyond one's ability to describe. It would put fear in people generally but excite the church in particular. This would be a part of the 'midnight cry' (Mt. 25:6) which will result in the wider awaking of the church. This will happen just before the Second Coming of Jesus (Mt. 25:10).

When Jews and Israelis en masse turn to Jesus in this way, does it mean that every single living Jew or Israeli will be saved? No. For not every Gentile was saved when the covenant privileges were offered to them. We therefore need not expect that every single Jew will be saved. Indeed, if the Greek word *pleroma* ('fullness') means 'full number', as the NIV translates Romans 11:25, it must also mean that in Romans 11:12, which would therefore refer to the full number of Jews. This means that there is a definite number of Gentiles who will be converted and a definite number of Jews. In either case it refers to the number of people who trust the blood of Jesus.

What will precede this 'life from the dead'? The hearing of the gospel by Jews and Israelis. Up to now they are generally described as spiritually blind and deaf (Rom. 11:8). But God will lift that blindness at some stage. How and when? I don't know. But it is not my problem. I only know that they need to *hear* the gospel and then see it clearly for themselves. When this happens it will be 'life from the dead'.

Three things I would say to the Israelis

I come now to three things I would choose to say, were I granted the privilege to address Israelis – whether it be in the Knesset, on television or to one Israeli at a time. I don't mind telling you I would go to the stake for this: what an honour to lay down my life after speaking this way. If I knew I would not get out of Israel alive I would say these things if given the opportunity. For either our gospel is true or it isn't. When Paul said to the Corinthians that he resolved to know nothing among them 'except Jesus Christ and him crucified' (1 Cor. 2:2), he meant that he decided to 'go for broke' – and put the greatest stigma there was before the Corinthians. After all, he knew they would never be saved until they heard that Jesus shed his blood on a cross (the worst stigma imaginable then and now), so why not be 'up front' with this from the start? Because I believe there is a heaven (where believers in Jesus go when they die) and a hell (where unbelievers go when they die), I would gladly lay down my life to see people brought to Jesus – wherever one had the privilege of speaking: in Jerusalem, New York, London or Ramallah. So these are the three things I would say to Israelis:

1. *God is trying to get Israel's attention*. The suicide bombings, the violence and the bloodshed that continue all over Israel are God's way of trying to get the attention of the Israelis – its leaders and everybody else. Peace will not come via a military or political solution. At the Dormitian Abbey I actually said, 'If they find Osama bin Laden, if the PLO find another leader, if there were a thousand Moshe Dayans to take over the armed forces, peace will elude you until you accept Jesus Christ as Messiah.' Sometimes the very thing God uses to get our attention is what initially puts us off him, but God stays with us until we bow the knee. It is because God still has a 'soft spot' for Israel that he allows adversity and calamity to thrive among his ancient people. He has always done this.

2. *Please look again at Isaiah 53 and Psalm 110*. Sadly, and oh how I wish this were not true, most Israelis

have not looked at Isaiah 53 even once. Most Israelis do not read their Bibles and do not realize what is said about Jesus, that right there in their Old Testament – Isaiah 53 – is what convinced Jews two thousand years ago that Jesus was indeed the promised Messiah. The most rational and simple understanding of Isaiah 53 is Jesus:

> He grew up before him like a tender shoot, and like a root out of dry ground. He had no beauty or majesty to attract us to him, nothing in his appearance that we should desire him. He was despised and rejected by men, a man of sorrows, and familiar with suffering. Like one from whom men hide their faces he was despised, and we esteemed him not. Surely he took up our infirmities and carried our sorrows, yet we considered him stricken by God, smitten by him, and afflicted. But he was pierced for our transgressions, he was crushed for our iniquities; the punishment that brought us peace was upon him, and by his wounds we are healed. We all, like sheep, have gone astray, each of us has turned to his own way; and the Lord has laid on him the iniquity of us all (Is. 53:2–6).

'The Lord says to my Lord: "Sit at my right hand until I make your enemies a footstool for your feet"' (Ps. 110:1). This is a Messianic psalm and shows in advance that the Messiah would ascend to the Father and sit at his right hand.

3. *Don't forget your real identity*. You are hated by your Middle Eastern neighbours not so much over what you have done but because of who you are. You are special. As Joseph's brothers hated him because he was Jacob's favourite, so the sons of Ishmael hate the people of Israel. The hostility is ancient, going back over 3,700 years.

There was Ishmael and then there was Isaac. Like it or not, God said to Abraham, the father of both of these boys, 'It is through Isaac that your offspring will be reckoned' (Gen. 21:12). That is when the hostility began and the reason it continues.

I would say to Israelis, who are your real friends in the world? Are they not the followers of Jesus? Why do you suppose the Corrie ten Booms of this world would risk their lives and hide Jews in the Second World War? One reason: because they were Jews – God's special people. The friends you have scattered throughout the world more often than not are followers of Jesus. Why? They know who you are! They know your real identity! I would plead on bended knee with every Israeli and every Jew, do not forget your identity. It goes back to Abraham, with whom God made a special covenant, and that alone is why God has a soft spot for you. It is my prayer that the blindness that is upon Israelis and Jews all over the world will soon be lifted so that you will have eyes to see and ears to hear. May God hasten the day.

Four days after I gave my talk at the Dormitian Abbey, the 250 Brits returned to the United Kingdom. On the same day, Lyndon Bowring and Alan Bell flew into Tel Aviv for a few days to relax. On Monday 1 July, Revd Andrew White flew into Israel. Julia Fisher told him about my conversation with Osama, the Palestinian driver.

Rais

I did not know that Canon Andrew White has the trust of both the Israeli government and Yasser Arafat. Andrew kindly passed on his mobile phone number to me and I phoned him at the time he suggested. There were a number of things that apparently made him interested in my meeting Arafat. First, the peace process was dead. Nothing was happening. But Andrew pointed out that, after all, is not the conflict basically religious? Therefore the Israelis seemed willing to try 'the religious track'. Secondly, he had just read my book *Total Forgiveness*; he seemed to know all about me and added that his own parents had attended our School of Theology at Westminster Chapel over the years. Third, I told him that I had begun praying daily for Yasser Arafat twenty years before as a result of things Arthur Blessitt told me about his time with Arafat. I was so gripped because of what Arthur told me, I could say I have prayed for Arafat hundreds and hundreds – even thousands – of times. Fourth, it was timely that an evangelical from the West would be willing to meet with Arafat at such a time as that, since President Bush had declared that Arafat should be replaced.

It was on 2 July that Andrew phoned us at our hotel in Tiberias. 'Yasser Arafat will see you tomorrow evening at 6 o'clock.' He added: 'You can bring one person with you.' I then had to look at Alan and Lyndon with this information and asked that they choose between them. We had to fax our passports immediately to the Israelis and happened to send all three, as it was not determined which one would go with me. It was decided that Lyndon would go, but when Andrew met Alan the next day and noticed that his passport too had been approved he said 'Both of you go – we will take two cars.' It was a wonderful moment, as I had felt horrible that Alan could not go with us. We met at our hotel in Jerusalem for an hour for some briefing. I was told to call Arafat by the title *Rais*, the Arabic word for president.

Space prevents me from describing the awesome sight of the checkpoints, the Israeli tanks with guns pointed at us, the sight of Ramallah and the conditions of Arafat's compound. We were shown into Arafat's room at 6 o'clock. He kissed me on both cheeks. 'I am honoured to meet you,' I said. 'Me too,' he replied. I was introduced to three of his cabinet ministers across the table. Arafat sat at the end of the table; Andrew White sat to my right – between Arafat and me. We were served glasses of mango juice. Arafat speaks good English but has a strong accent and I had to listen carefully.

Alan and Lyndon remained silent during the entire one hour and forty-five minutes. But Alan kept his right hand on my back, praying silently, and Lyndon did the same with Alan. I took their advice – as well as that of Louise when I phoned her to say I would be meeting Arafat: 'Smile. Look pleasant.' I need that kind of advice all the time, I'm afraid. In any case, I felt tremendous liberty – as great an anointing as I have ever known in any pulpit – as I spoke to the PLO Chairman and his three ministers. Once Andrew and Arafat had finished with some brief business, Andrew nodded for me to speak.

'I cannot prove this, *Rais*, but I think I have probably prayed for you more than any church leader in the world,' I began. He seemed very touched by this. 'It is because a man by the name of Arthur Blessitt who carries a cross . . .'

He interrupted me. 'Look,' he said, pointing to a small cross (perhaps two inches long) that Arthur had carved for Arafat from the wood of his own cross. Arthur was thrilled when I later told him that Arafat keeps that little cross on his desk. 'I gave him that in Gaza,' Arthur said, which shows that Arafat took pains to keep it with him.

'I would not want you to underestimate the importance of this visit,' I continued. 'I do not come as a politician but as a follower of Jesus Christ.' His comment and facial expression conveyed the impression that he was most certainly not underestimating the importance of my visit.

I said to him 'Jesus loves you.' He rolled his eyes toward the ceiling. I could see that this did not impress him too much. Five minutes later I said 'I want you to know that I admire you and that I love you.' At that moment tears filled his eyes. It was almost as though we bonded. 'I have come today to be Jesus to you,' I added.

'Our Koran says that Jesus went to heaven,' he said – as if I might be impressed at this.

'Not good enough,' I replied. 'You do not believe that *he died* first. If you were to see that Jesus *died* – and was raised from the dead and then went to heaven, you would be given supernatural wisdom.' His eyes moistened again.

One of the Palestinian cabinet ministers entered into the conversion. 'We believe that Jesus was a prophet.'

'Not good enough,' I countered again. 'He was the Son of God.'

President Arafat got up from his chair and walked over to me with his Koran. He turned to a certain place and laid it before my eyes. 'Look at this,' he said to me (as if I could read Arabic). 'Did you know that the only woman mentioned in the Koran was the Virgin Mary?' I think he thought this would impress me. But I replied 'Well now, isn't that interesting? That proves Jesus was the Son of God because he had no earthly father.' Arafat went back and sat down but did not seem at all offended.

I wanted to speak into his pain and the plight of Palestinians at the time.

'I am sorry for what you have been through,' I said to him.

'Sixty-six thousand of our people have been killed,' he replied.

'Jesus did not do that to you. Jesus would not do that to you. That has been done to you by a people who also need to recognize Jesus as their Messiah, *Rais*, but Jesus would never do that to you.' He nodded as if he completely agreed with me.

'Jesus knew what it was to suffer and be rejected,' said Arafat. 'Yes,' I replied, 'a bruised reed he would not break. I have come to be Jesus to you today,' I said again.

I asked Arafat if he would sign my Bible. I showed him that King Hussein of Jordan had also signed it. Arafat signed my Bible in English and Arabic right next to the signature of King Hussein. Since the two were not close friends I think that would make that page in my Bible somewhat rare, added to which I have the signature of Moishe Rosen, the founder of Jews for Jesus, just above that of King Hussein! I avoided politics, however. The nearest we came to that was when he mentioned President Jimmy Carter. I suggested he write to the former president. I carried a letter from Arafat to Jimmy Carter across the Atlantic and mailed it. In it he asked the former president if he would please come and supervise the coming Palestinian elections.

I made a point – perhaps six times – during our time together in order to stress that Jesus *died*. A Muslim will not admit that Jesus died on the cross, only that he was delivered from the cross and ascended to heaven. Knowing this, I kept pressing this home. '*Rais*, affirm that Jesus *died* and you will be given supernatural wisdom.'

When it appeared that we would shortly be ending our time together, I asked if I could read from the Bible and pray. Arafat nodded affirmatively. I read Psalm 133 and John 3:16. When I read the words 'He gave his one and only Son', I added 'who *died*'. I then looked at him and said 'The most important question anybody can ask you is, "Where will you be one hundred years from now?" I have one hope of going to heaven. I have transferred my trust in my good works to what Jesus did for me on the cross – Jesus who *died*.' He then looked at me as if to say that he got my point!

I asked if I could lead in prayer. Yes. I prayed for Yasser Arafat and also for the three cabinet ministers across the table. I prayed that they would all see that Jesus died for them and asked specifically for Arafat 'Cover him by the blood of Jesus.' I opened my eyes. His eyes were closed.

I then gave a little prophecy to Arafat. 'The day will come, *Rais*, when there will be so many Israelis converted to Christ that they will say to you Palestinians "Is it the Temple Mount you want? Take it. You can have it. We've found something better. Two thousand years ago the veil of the temple was ripped in two from top to bottom when Jesus died on the cross. We have found the real thing." Then you Palestinians will say to the Israelis "We never thought we would hear you talk like that. We want what you've got." And then there will be peace in Jerusalem. But not before.'